Alexandra Kraeler Corbin

Published by Red Roof Press, Poughquag, NY 12570

Conversion Devices

Alexandra K. Corbin

To the human brain.

Hopefully indefatigable and

hopelessly imitative.

CONTENTS

Conversion Devices

Conversion Devices

PART ONE

Imitation. It sounds so simple at the get-go. Yet our 'imaging impulse,' that which ignites our production of freestanding designs and the subject of this investigation, begins with it. The concept of mimicry in any form and by any means drives all of our behaviors as it does for most other animals. For many scholars, the big question is how much is built in and how much is advertised or taught. Here is where I demure because this question is definitely not the subject of this book, and I suggest there are other and perhaps even bigger non-Darwinian questions at play (One might want to consider the work of Alfred Russell Wallace, who takes a far more balanced approach than Darwin did).

As an artist, I am infinitely perplexed and rather amazed by the routines of mimesis. How is it that a mark made on paper, for example, ever so sloppily or slightly referring to a shape visualized with eyes open or closed, carries the insignia of that entity? There must be an intrinsic mapping device that is highly catholic at accepting categorical configurations. But it does have regulations. Our brains know when

1

that catholic willingness to make sense of things just throws up its hands in exasperation and says, 'No way!

These days, neuro-psychology labs are humming with experiments to test the limits and formation of these regulations. But artists have always been testing just how indulgent our brains are. We were the first scientists, perhaps? We fiddle with the outer regions of recognition paradigms all the time. And we ask for more and more leniency, knowing all along that there has to be a point of no return, when the collected elements like lines or dots, what have you, just never convince. This is usually when you see more words spill forth from the artist or critic in the absence of visual conviction. Every time I sit down to fabricate an image/object, I am prodding and poking at those regulations.

However, in primitive societies, where the functional linkage is supreme, this kind of intellectual mischief is relatively absent. By functional, I do not mean how to make a poi pounder more effective in its ability to macerate, but rather how efficiently the image links beliefs with expectations about their world. Human perception is a balancing act of minimizing surprise, another word for entropy or chaos. Chaos is a huge negative, which is why all of us and all animals strive to expend the least amount of energy in maintaining equilibrium.

We set rules of perception, which is an inner model for the world based on a combination of beliefs that is reinforced by sensations. Karl Friston describes:

> '...the brain (as) an inference machine that actively predicts and explains sensations...a probalistic model that can generate predictions against which sensory samples are tested to update beliefs about their causes' (Friston 2010:3).

2

'Conviction' is the name of the game. This is the power to most swiftly define and prescribe expectations about the world to channel sensations effectively and apply them to our preexisting formatting about the environment. Conviction is as relevant in private carvings as it is for public imagery. By 'private' I mean the kind that are intended just for the satisfaction of the maker and are often expelled, destroyed, buried, and abandoned. This might help explain why so many thematic 'cultural' designs, both private and public, endure through the ages. If they have been convincing and well-known, why mess with success?

What we are really asking is how can our physical gestures, which themselves are really abstract movements, convert cerebral notions into convincing interpretations of our world? There is much at work here, but one remarkable part is our cognitive devotion to always making sense of independent gestures or markings by aggregating them into collections.

One 'thing' is insufficient. Two 'things' ask us to affirm linkages as meaningful. As intentional. It is a kind of naïve belief that everything we combine together, in other words, or that we make or discern *must be* a pointer, a cognitive index finger. And a pointer that not only asks us to concentrate, but also de rigueur, points backward to its causes. If we didn't have this mentality for causality with attention, which is taught very early on, we would be subject to chaos, and I wouldn't be writing this now because there would never have been a sustainable species to begin with.

Humans simply cannot let things lie unresolved. We just can't. But stubbornness alone, perhaps even arrogance that we always cobble purposefulness for anything we do, is insufficient for a complex chain of cognitive operations. 'Meaning' is *ex post facto* and comes well after what appears instinctive because those synaptic operations that result in creativity are so fluid. These are operations that are intended to capture (i.e., tangibly convert impressions or ideas), the completely non-substantive stuff of cognition. Gestures must somehow be harnessed, organized, and guided to convert the ephemeral neural 'stuff' physically into solid and detached references. In this case, 'art,' but in all other cases, freestanding forms.

I determined that there are classifiable responses that drive our instinct to peg ideas to forms. Or better still, to bridge an interior motive with an exterior effect. I call these **'conversion devices.'**

Broadly, they are novelty, intention, mirroring and recursion. Although these appear to be behavioral, even psychological, responses, they are deeply neural idiosyncrasies that appear innate, albeit abetted by nurturing. Each will be addressed individually as best as they can because they interface with each other and are difficult to separate. Extirpate one and it collapses the function of the other.

We shall lead the discussion through behaviors that reveal just how dynamic these devices truly are. But the remarkable revelation is that all of them exercise contiguous neural loci around the premotor cortex and Pars Opercularis, a part of the brain identified by Korbinian Brodmann as area 44 (Binkofski 2000; Heiser 2003; Vaina 2001). Even more fascinating is that it's an area long ago, and still rather narrowly, defined as an exclusive driver for verbal language formulation (as opposed to production).

Clearly it is not. But these loci of which each brain has two, are also significant for evolution of perspectives, especially the projection of the self as a third-party observer in the role of the actor (Shipton 2009; Tomasello 1999; Iacobini 2003; Rizzolatti 1996). This means that 'I' am the first party, observing someone else, the second party, and then inject my idea of self into that second party and imagine seeing myself as if it were me instead of them. I am an actor because I am role playing but also observing myself in that role. It is here where the 'likeness' or mimetic concept resides in its starkest incarnation.

4

It sounds awfully convoluted, which it certainly is. But it is a fluid conversion that humans undertake with the greatest of ease, both automatically and self-consciously. The most self-conscious industry being those of the creative arts, but also more mundanely, for all manufactured objects we use that others also have such as smartphones and fashion trends.

The Pars Opercularis is curious. And we suggest that perspective swapping, which is the fundamental driver of mimesis, is generated here. It is likely a behavior as innate and essential to binding us in communities as any basic survival habit could possibly be. If the neural clusters that instigate this interpolation of oneself as another object were less robust or absent, communication on any level would be highly unlikely.

In contrast, it is often said that for autists, this kind of Theory of Mind (ToM) never reverberates beyond the personal body. For them, the simulation of otherness is often a sense that parts of their own body and mind are those other foreign, third-party things. It is a dialogue that rages and enrages within their corporeal walls, a dialogue that is often characterized as their 'thinking self versus their feeling self' (Grandin 2013).

***

Let's return to what might underlie a signature of our species, one that is not unlike other animals such as canines and corvid birds, even ants. We are manic obsessive collectors. It represents a fundamental effect of the need for mimesis and a primitive means by which we convert ideas to forms.

Now just think about what a collection is. It is an entity defined by its parts. Well, not so fast. It's an entity defined differently from its signature parts. Whether it's a compost pile from your garbage, your bedroom closet, or your flash file. We know there's a lot of good stuff on that file so the file or little metal 'thing' becomes a safety net for good facts, though we hardly know what they all are. But those parts taken alone are insufficient entities themselves. Collections have conviction. It is not 'the more the merrier.' It is 'the more the louder.'

This collecting activity reminds me of the old stories of vampires haunting Eastern European grave sites. The adage was that to keep these predators away, all you needed to do was sprinkle rice (grains, seeds, and anything, really). Their obsession to arrange and collect would halt their pursuit of carrion long enough for them to sit down and count every last kernel. Then, if you go to the cemetery in Montmartre, Paris, you'll see a curious sight on all the Jewish graves. You might also see a family member refreshing its 'protection' by piling on rather nice, stubby-sized, rounded, river pebbles. Forget the symbolic trickle-down narratives about weighting down souls, about sacrifices, about stones as hearts and connecting with god.

The resemblance to all apotropaic counting distractions is too obvious to be overlooked, and you can be sure that originally these customs derived from the same source—to distract by enticing the predator, deity, or otherwise with collections to be counted. What does it tell us about human behavior?

Our recognition system is designed the same way in a mania to first sit down and organize and collect all the disparate kernels into a unique figure; in their case, a specific number of seeds, and in ours, a specificity of an identity. Often this is called 'coalition,' a vague term. And it requires 'computation,' another favorite scientific term for thinking through to an identification. Nevertheless, the dynamic is irresistible. It is an addiction. For some reason, there is just too much invested in it. But what exactly drives this? The answer is ourselves, each hard-working, individual brain, naturally.

When speaking of identification paradigms—sometimes called explicit or implicit categories—the usual scientific machinery tends to be sought in the temporal and occipital visual systems, which begin as shape or color or object networks. Though coalescing these elements into generalized imagery (i.e., implicit) and from there into specific remembered identities (i.e., explicit) is just personal habits.

Even (cognitive) styles are ability-based, as Maria Kozhevnikov maintains, who has designed her fair share of perception tests. Many ascribe the former, implicit, as often characterized by requiring more mental computation because the reference or symbol (I prefer to avoid this word) is latent and requires more information to incorporate into your purposeful thinking than an explicit one does.

I am uncertain of this. The separation of these into imagery typing is certainly not the originating motivation for visualizing. Though many would say, 'Ah, but to survive, we need to process fast. We need both.' To which I answer, 'True, but that is psychologically driven. It is additive, conditional, accretive, and manageable. And all of this based on experience.' And what motivates us in the first place to sculpt experience into these nice recognition patterns is very likely something else.

No, it begins in that 'something or somewhere else' domain before it can ever get to those efficiently humming, efficiency recognition systems. And that somewhere else both *is* and *feeds* a neuro-psychological hunger for 'acting' out, as in impersonating.

The most important concept of mimicry is the application of oneself as the unique uber-tool, much like a tensile pen, by which to draft the world as we sense it. In effect, we don't require other tools or meta tools to extend our sensory and interpretative reach; all we need is the neural textile of interwoven sensations as they issue upsweeping unities called ideas or responses that extend through our bodies on through our orifices, surfaces, limbs, and then outwards to the tip of a little finger or toe (generally). We can harness these to mechanical extenders like charcoal, computers, hammers, and selfie sticks, but we are the essential meta tool.

How does a rush of spiking synapses translate into a gross-motor, physical action that refers directly to the initiating neural impulse? Here's the answer: I don't know. Nevertheless, keep reading.

The Pointer

All of us, beginning in infancy, extend the index finger to point to objects that excite. You never see them do it with a thumb, and for good neural reasons (i.e., mechano-receptors), discussed in previous chapters. When you see an artist or anyone use his thumb, it is as a 'volume' extender or 'volume carver,' as if running your hand along a surface to feel physical edges and implicit volumes. It is more sensual than the index finger, which I like to think is more intellectual.

Why do I say this? Because the index finger is this little drawing or outlining tool that physically converts those upsweeping ideas about colored shapes issued from the brain. It is a conversion device in real-time, physical action. Just pointing your finger is essentially telling 'you' that 'you' have determined a collection of colors to be confined into a unique specificity. The index finger signals our decisions about what spots of color to coalesce into usable and recognizable forms. It emphasizes that the brain firmly believes it can reach out and touch that 'thing.' And this in turn requires us to invent a complete abstract boundary around it. Thus, our little finger becomes the most universal mechanical conversion device and uber-tool we possess.

But how can there be borders around mist and color fields, and the mellifluous flow of swirls and hues? Well, shapes of any variety are collections of dots and nuances and trends that eventually fall off and become something else in our mind's eye. And humans don't much care to stand around enjoying this lack of resolution. We despise confusion.

Instead, we seek where the fall-off can best be determined so we can move our brains off to more urgent matters. We make definitions out of a mess. And we make decisions, for better or worse, about ambiguities and nuance.

Homo Sapiens by virtue of our name are discerning of many things. We are 'thing-ists'. We necessarily have *border* mentalities and not necessarily because our optical system is prone to this, which it definitely is. One could take the statement above about border mentalities and run with it in psycho-sociological terms about nations and wars.

Nevertheless, 'Sapiens' really means knowing 'about' or around or concerning something by determining where to set the limits and circumscribe 'it.' That is all. The word 'Sapiens' is an active term, a gerund.

It confers on our species the constant activity of seeking knowledge in every breathing moment. 'Knowing' is an abstract concept. Highly illusive. Frustrating. And breathlessly enticing. It has extreme limitations that manifest in the irreconcilable differences between materials; that one molecular structure, namely ourselves, simply cannot naturally 'read' or align with the molecular components of a differing one.

Thus, we can only circle or know 'about', around, or regarding something. This is why for humans about other humans, we require communication systems to try to figure each other out. Each of us is a different material structure. These constructs such as verbal language are faulty and irritating, but they are all we have to 'know about' each other and things. In effect, we employ them to circumscribe a collection of parts, assets, activities, etc. as unique among so many other moving parts on the universal stage.

And this is also why humans adore lines.

By the way, a line is a very definite kind of shape. Its dimension being defined mostly by a width considerably less than its length. That's all. And depending on where you are standing, the proportions change dramatically. It's a relativity thing. A portion of a line can be enormous, say, for an ant on a stick or for a human fording the Grand Canyon, which is a linear gash in the earth.

Right off the bat, I would have to say that even though our fancy visual system as intimately revealed by Torsten Wiesel and David Hubel, which sorts light through a retinal contrast system of edges into inclined lines and curves, truly are not linear inclinations; they are shapes. A true line in my mind is non-existent. The best that can be said is as an impression of where boundaries collide rather than as a freestanding edge.

What is a freestanding edge? Think about it. No edge can be absolutely freestanding. It is a possessive, belonging to something else, always. So, I can't go shopping for boundaries. I can't pick them up and collect them without lifting up a host of other entities they divide. 'Lines' exist in our brains and not in reality. Though the concept is utterly diabolic because we are contour freaks and invent something that isn't there.

We constantly invent 'separators.' A shifting reality of sorts that jockeys between and among things and never has a life of its own. This is a concept not an entity. Yet every second of our living is mentally devoted to this.

Anyway, you can still translate all of this 'separation anxiety' with the little pointer index finger. It isolates boundaries by identifying an object. You can also do this with your far clumsier big toe when it draws in the mud or sand. And if need be, we can do 'it' with any other part of our body, surrendering the control and incredible detail work of the index finger. We can delineate with elbows, knees, noses, and more.

We can even delineate with our entire body as in dance and athletics. In all of these, we leave whisper lines, the instantaneous memory of a motion continues to whisper for a few more moments. It is enough for our brain to connect the whispers by drafting them into a fluid line in our mind's eye. But it is evident and best seen when we skate or when we walk in wet sand. The track is clear. You, we, get the picture.

***

Animals 'copycat,' apprentice. They follow the leader by swarming (i.e., mass follow-the-leader behaviors) and through nurturing. But we use the full gamut of our corporeal gifts to attempt something quite arrogant because it is virtually impossible to really do—to elide with everything in our ken as if *we* personally have no boundaries, no strict defining contour lines, as if we were some kind of magical shape/form *meister*. There's beautiful irony here if you accept what seems to be counterintuitive. At first, you'd think that if we are so decisive, better still, argumentative, about borders and objects then we should have a kneejerk understanding about what monolithic place each thing rightfully occupies. Especially ourselves.

Think again. The fact is that if we are so used to making those determinations from on high, from inside our minds, then why stop there? If we cognitively set the limits on all these things, we are imperiously 'knowing all about' all these things. We believe we can embrace their full existence. Therefore, we seem to be talking about something that begins with the notion of empathy as in to 'feel your pain.' But it goes further. It encompasses the belief, a directive from the brain again, that 'I am that' or certainly could be on any level of our choosing. I can be a steel girder when I draw one. At least I think I can mimic one. And that is all that matters.

Circumscribing 'Me'

It is very simple to say, 'Of course, we aren't.' I am not a bug nor am I the sky in physiological terms. No. We are wrapped up tightly with a layer of dermis and the only thing we 'give off' that molecularly melds with the life around us is the air we breathe out, the smells and tissues we shed, and the sounds and vibrations we utter and mutter. Perhaps also, the air we displace, the heat we radiate, and the electricity we generate. But we do not morphologically commingle with anything else.

Though at this point it is appropriate and certainly fun to inject the universal beliefs of 'spirit' as being at once pervasive yet separate, vaporous and immortal. Best explained by the Ancient Egyptians, the most significant components are the 'Ba,' 'Sheut,' and 'Ib.' The 'Ba' is the personality, 'Sheut' your shadow, and 'Ib' the conceptual heart as in the seat of emotions, intention, and freewill. Of the three, the most brilliant and legitimate claimant to the objectification of an ego influencing the environment would have to be the 'Sheut.'

As your shadow, this is a fascinating shape that follows and precedes you through life. It obscures other 'things' by blocking reflected light quanta of objects and has a diabolic, if not utterly quixotic, mind of its own by engorging and shrinking and changing contour throughout the day if not also through one's life. So let's add 'sheut' in there with electromagnetism, sound, and heat. For we truly do alter the atomic structure of things when we skew light waves.

Aside from these, everything we might attempt regarding melding our corporeal selves with anything else is highly poetic. So, since we cannot absolutely flow into and become everything under the sun by means of transformations like Merlin, we reluctantly have to settle and do it by copying.

A Perfect Likeness

In our minds, many animals can seemingly flow into and merge with their environments and by so doing, become cryptic, meaning camouflaged and hidden. To avoid their predators, we find startlingly amazing color and size tricks. The list is enormous for bugs and snakes that mask themselves by mimicking the color and patterns of their host object, like a tree or sand. Every child knows about chameleon transformations. Called 'crypsis,' the king of all these magicians would have to be (at least for me) the cephalopod, which Italians adore munching. The incredible octopus.

Let's briefly dip under water and see how it finesses escape from danger in its dark beyond. As you read through, keep in mind what humans are limited to doing as opposed to what they can invent in their fashion to escape predation. Also, keep in mind that escaping predators often means you best become one.

The octopus has superior vision, stereoscopic in fact. It can discern the differences between 3D as in its own active environment versus a flat photograph. All of its color, texture, size, and locomotive mimicry originates as inputs to its brain, which then determines which of the chromatophores (i.e., color pigmented cells) and reflecting cells to turn on. These range in hue from black through orange and yellow to violets, pinks, blues, and silvers. It can mimic textures or papillations, from smooth to pebbly. And even more remarkable, doing it without 'touching' the other objects, merely by its 3D interpolations. It can sway in the water imitating sea weed or posture itself in the sand so compressed as to be, well, flattened like a flounder.

Humans can do all of this and none of this. When we input our seeing codes to the brain, we can't physically transform our bodies accordingly. So, what do we clumsy biped creatures do? Darwin's gracious competitor and admirer Alfred Russell Wallace gives us a clue in his famous Ternate Essay (1858 *'On the Tendency of Varieties to Depart Indefinitely from the Original Type'*).

> ...a deficiency in one set of organs (is) always being compensated by an increased development in others...

It could be said that we sprouted some amazing capacities in our brains as a form of compensation, and that compensation is best manifested by mimicry inventions. Though we can't turn shades of blue, we sure do invent tools to disguise ourselves. Even blue makeup if need be. Though lately, *The Blue Man Group* has pretty much cornered that market.

Masquerading with feathers, costumes, and pigments comprise our color and textural mimicry if, for example, we want to enroll in a herd of seals or gazelles to get closer for the kill. Or just to observe. Think about it, if we really wanted that much to be a ballyhooed fly on the wall, we'd pretty much figure out how to camouflage ourselves with an overall covering that obscured our form or distracted others with some kind of jamming device.

This certainly helps in combat, where our soldiers wear camouflage clothes to hide in all varieties of brush and natural patterns. We owe this iconic military attire to the great *camofleurs* of France during World War I, who were tasked with inventing 'dazzle' designs based on the cubist works of George Braque and Pablo Picasso. Mimicking logs, disguising boat hulls, painting canvases (and frescoes) in *trompe l'oeil*, all trick some predator's eye.

Much of this 20th-century obsession was due to a wakeup call from the American artist Abbot Thayer, whose 1909 book '*Concealing Coloration in the Animal Kingdom,*' converged so nicely with the deconstructing visualizations of the French painters mentioned above. It was a period in our intellectual development during which artists, especially during the post-impressionist period, had led the way to analyzing the nature of seeing and how the brain reconstructs abstract data into recognition.

But humans had long been doing this. Maybe we had always been doing this. I suggest we had, and that it is the reason we are still around today.

We had to invent fakery since we lacked the natural assets of other animals and their fabulous cellular arrays. As a result, we invented mimicry by inventing fabrications. If we teach children to 'Find Waldo,' we also teach in the same breath how to slip out of your identity and get lost in a crowd. What was the point of sneaking up on an elk if we looked different? We assumed the elk could see us with the same discretionary brain as we had. We needed a headdress that mimicked an elk's head, and couple that with the right kind of choreography. We started to 'think that we could think' like an elk by deciding what seeing like an elk might be like. In our thoughts, we swapped identities and imagined ourselves in the role of elk long before we ever picked up so much as a feather to build a mask.

Where along this progression one draws the line between tools and art is almost a ridiculous determination. It's quite ridiculous. But it explains why so many theorists, critics, and academics feel a constant need to ascribe 'meaning' as the *modus operandi* for the art impulse today. Instead, consider that 'Meaning' is a more theoretical take on the concept of utility. It is the 'because' part of the clause, 'We do this *because* we need to eat.' The meaning of the activity is 'needing to eat.'

We come up with the explanations to justify an unexplainable impulse. I am suggesting that all of us tend to read the effect as the cause and that is giving the devil too much due. Might what is meaningful not at all be the effect nor the impetus? Perhaps there's something far more basic, far more urgent, and far more agitating that underscores the first part of that sentence—the 'doing' of it. And perhaps as Wallace suggested, we are compensating for a deficiency in some organ(s) by increasing use of another.

Let's wonder for a moment whether the inherent assumption and operating motivation is the goal of capturing a 'perfect likeness.' Not to fake out elk, or enemies, or spy on others. In fact, for no apparent reason at all. Do we and other animals attempt to ape aspects of our environment, including group members, and believe that we have the wherewithal to replicate perfectly in identical form and substance what we think we sense is there? This presumes a lot.

Unfortunately, we humans never seem to take it in stride. We agitate over this. We envy. We compete. And envy again. Intellectually, the job is ongoing.

Here is where we differ from the octopus. You see, imitation is the most frustrating gambit a human ever takes on. When we so-called artists have a creative 'block,' it is at root an imitation failure of goal and method. Yet even with the newest tools like scanning high def and photography, our goal to capture perfectly is still quixotic. It is impossible to constrain the likeness of things fully in a static storage system. Ergo, the remarkable tsunami of Instagram photos, the looping of videos, etc. Were we to 'get it right' from the get-go, we wouldn't require tools that help us make so many passes at the same thing. 'Much,' 'many,' and 'more' attempts do not seem to get the work done. Nothing satisfies. It's sort of close 'but no cigar.'

Life goes by too fast and these incredibly clever devices in the end are so flatfooted. Sixth-, seventh-, eighth-generation (8g) technology notwithstanding, this is frustration number one. But it is also the addiction of coming so close to the reality of the moment. And moments comprise non-tangibles such as anxiety and joy and other contexts so subtle but that color up all of our sensations and actions. Call it the prosody of reality.

Having been in academia and art, I can say there is nothing more mentally exhausting, woefully frustrating yet rewarding as this copyist challenge. We might fiddle with the procedures. We may use at times silly and at times brilliant newfangled meta-tools like using one tool to use another like a rod to dangle a hook. But we are still using the joints in our elbows to the tip of our fingers, even the jaws of our mouths, to extend the impulses from our brain in order to manipulate the placements of these corporeal meta-tools.

The Crux of the Matter

Humans set a ridiculously high bar for 'likeness' productions. Consider that we are now down to cubic pixels called voxels in MRIs to capture the implied three-dimensional likeness of neurons, not to mention the scans and graphs of sub-atomic particles. The crux of the matter is that it can't have been too high a bar because we have traveled so vast a distance from our beginnings obsessively pursuing this. As has often been posited, the tools appear to have outpaced our ability to absorb their use and ramifications, all of which takes time.

Determinists would say, and with good reason, that if we can 'do' something then, it was genetically programmed in us to be able to do so in the first place. And the use of these tools, however newfangled, will be fully absorbed in due course without altering our essential behaviors.

Right now, in the early stages of its use, the Internet and social media has as much downside as upside. There is a FOMO (fear of missing out) anxiety that roils so many young minds. It bands them into lemming mentalities of 'loser versus winners,' perhaps with even far more perplexing and negative complications yet to be defined. So, we are in our evolutionary infancy regarding this particular 'likeness tool,' as we must have been when we discovered how to light a fire and scratch a line and repeatedly yell the same warning sounds.

The point being that we keep lurching toward facsimile by means of collecting enough information to capture for good what something or other really is. Therein lies the rub. 'Facsimile' means identical replication in the same medium. But I am not a tree. Nor is my life at this moment fully described by the algorithms of a Facebook page. Mimicry is the best we can deliver and always in other media. If so, why this constant yearning for it? Are we intentionally kidding ourselves?

The Dead Cat

Certainly, we are not dumb and we have conscious understanding for the breadth of procedure required to do anything, especially once we stop to think about it. If you think about walking, it could become an unpleasant balancing act. People rarely do stop and think about these natural behaviors. However, there is one thing we know for certain; we cannot perfectly replicate something in our heads. The natural procedure itself sabotages it. And thinking about it makes it even worse.

Much like *Schrödinger's Cat*, the minute we penetrate and try to 'capture' the closed ideated unit let's say of a thought for example or even an event which means in location and time, the totality collapses. Intercepting a thought necessarily destroys it to some degree and certainly ascertaining its placement collapses its time placement. As a result, we simply cannot attempt to invade, or merge with something else without ushering in the toxic fumes of putting that something else completely in our own personal time and space spectrum. Even if that something else wholly belongs to us because it originates in our brains. But let's steer clear of philosophically laced rhetoric and keep it really simple. The minute we attempt to penetrate a closed system like an uninvited guest crashing someone else's family dinner, the proceedings become immediately tainted and discordant, and collapse in un-choreographed chaos. The thought sputters. The cat dies.

To process something all the way through, from conception to acting it out, is like that too. Thus, we stumble over any aspirations to a 'perfect likeness' because it is, in fact, an oxymoron, a built-in excuse for trying and always failing. After all, 'perfect' is the opposite of something that falters and is 'like' something else. To get from 'likeness' to 'perfect' means boldly, or stubbornly, fording enormous chasms of interpretations, mis-readings, errors, and substantive inefficiencies based on sensory habits and material differences that are mutually exclusive.

The distance traversed in the processing itself collapses the 'perfection' of the initial trigger, that infernal 'cat in the box.' Check if the cat just might have died and you tamper with the perfectly balanced, albeit tenuous, environment. Now the animal will certainly be asphyxiated. Check out the path of a single photon shot through two minute pinholes onto a screen and you interfere with its absolute intention. Intercept an idea of a beautiful face by trying to drill down on details like lips, and the whole image disappears. It cannot be recovered perfectly as first conceived. We hope you try doing it. It is incredibly frustrating.

Media

There are 'many a slip twixt the cup and the lip' since we can only capture sensations in our faulty, restrictive, analog, sensory limitations. The following builds on the discussion of the previous chapters regarding the emotional and narrative investment we make when taming the insouciance of 'mystery' in our daily lives. Herein, we shall explore some of the more mechanical means by which humans mediate imitation responses, both automatic and volitional, and how we convert these corporeal sensitivities into extraneous objects.

A cautionary note: I fully accept that an idea constitutes a corporeal *sensitivity* too. Therefore, we discuss what these cognitive 'media' are. A good trick to keep in mind is to understand that 'media' is short for that which 'intermediates' or pulls something halfway to something else. It always implies 'between things' whence it derives its incredible power to influence and alter.

However, a conversion device alters substances. A frying pan molecularly alters a slimy raw egg. Think of it as a passage or vehicle by which one thing gets converted to another, like the dove becoming a rabbit in a magician's hat. The hat intermediates. Or at least seems to, but that's good enough. What then are the human magic hats by which we convert light quanta into visualizations and then in turn convert these to touchable forms that can be revisited over time? What, for example, intermediates a visualization into 'art,' let alone an object, and what in turn does art mediate? To answer this, we first must address a simple but always overlooked behavior.

To Revisit Something

When we copy and imitate, aren't we really doing so to revisit something? Doesn't this also mean that we are essentially collecting as well?

For example, doesn't *revisit* mean something by which you collect experiences as in to touch or maneuver or respond to on a variety of levels like handling a piece of jewelry or looping a song or viewing a flat image from different angles and at different times? Each case represents a collection of feedback from a single event. Most would obviously agree this is true. But couldn't the idea of revisiting also mean something to be remembered or referenced even just once more beyond the initial introduction, often by means of a context that triggers this very recent memory pathway?

That was certainly far too long-winded. Here's a short form: If I have just looked at a bull's eye, am I momentarily more sensitive to circular forms? How long does this 'imprint' (or prompt) last? The fact is that no one really knows since each circumstance differs.

Our brain has a system for revisiting through memory applications of different intensities. What is called visual short-term memory (VSTM) has a normal lifeline of at least seconds. Depending on the *intention* of the individual, these scenes or objects can be retained in some form despite refocusing on other disruptions as long as something else 'memorable' does not immediately occlude it. These 'cues' and prompts are incredibly sly. There is no real way to determine how they interweave throughout the brain because the levels of attention from salient to noteworthy to field dependent, meaning their inadvertent circumstantial participation, make tracks of one degree or another. By the way, you can go ahead and plug in the word 'attention' for 'intention.' You cannot *intend* something without a decision to focus on it. They are pretty much the same thing, not completely, but good enough. If I pay attention to a flower, it is because slightly preceding doing so it was my intention to do so over other distractions.

And of course, there are many levels of intention. Your teenage son cannot 'hear' you no matter how many times you repeat a request or how loudly you do so. Call it an intentional 'blind spot.' What is remarkable and needs to be applied to visualizations is that some level of your demand does get through. If you have asked him to take the dog out five times, an hour later you might discover that he emptied the garbage. Something penetrated and diffused in his brain, though his intention was minimal, and that's being generous.

Similarly, the likelihood is of VSTM acting in the same way, that it has a longer-term effect than we can possibly determine at this point. Anecdotal applications are worth consideration. For example, there are many of us who train ourselves in remembering 'prompts,' like the artist James A. M. Whistler.

I admit I refer to him a good deal because I respect him tremendously and he was such a colorful character. A truly honest artist trying so hard to understand what was really in front of his eyeballs and therefore, his brain, he was at odds with many of his humanist contemporaries. Even his creative process was one of digging deeper into the world of seeing than merely copying like a human caliper. He destroyed or scraped out more than other artists. He was perpetually frustrated.

Whistler was academically trained to close his eyes and remember the object/scene immediately. Then sketch it. He continued this exercise on his own throughout his life. I do so myself more and more. But it remains a very difficult exercise because humans are cognitive crumb trackers. We always move on to pick up the next information crumb along the path. The temptations are fierce to discard the old and collect the new inputs. Whistler's frustration was in capturing the first impression and to extend what was 'then' into an ever presence. How long could he extend his VSTM? He was in every way, the first impressionist.

Luckily in everyday life the prompts or cues are reinforced by the very designs we proliferate in our daily lives. They act like public billboards to keep reminding us of our visual short-term memories. If we just saw a bull's eye, that image resounds longer than a mere second or so because there are so many other circular patterns and designs that infiltrate our visual field at any given moment. Cups, letters, hats, emblems, light bulbs, rings, the edge of my cuffs, and I'm just naming the few I see right now in my little cubby that is so-called Spartan. This enables us to shuttle VSTM into some kind of long-term memory that helps feed our pigeonholing of icons.

In a study by Griffin and Nobre in 2005 and in the work of many, many others it has been found, 'Compared with no-cue trials, cuing attention to the potential target increases memory performance.' In 2003, Rogier Landman and his associates tried to confirm that retroactively flagging an item in our VSTM increases our sensitivity for change detection. Meaning we are alert to minor scenic changes from one moment to the next and can name that change. Also, that we store this fleeting knowledge in some cortical hub that he labeled a 'cortical icon,' a kind of icon potential.

Think about it, everything we see and do is a form of the same, isn't it? If you see a pattern on the skirt of a passerby and think about that pattern even for a nanosecond after you turned your eyes away, which you cannot help but do in some infinitesimal capacity, can't it be said that you are still 'revisiting' or retroactively flagging it? Scientific experiments and articles are rife with this concept of priming as a means to pry the innate habits of neural loci. But you don't need a PhD to know it's our *modus operandi*.

*

Memory itself is re-collective, though in a rather odd way. Here's why. To mentally re-collect or revisit, you first have to reconstitute. And you simply cannot 'purely' or perfectly do this given the organic and fluid contextualizing that defines what living is. You are changing every second, and with that go your sensations, your priorities, your influences, your prompts, and your stories. And your short-term memories. But the answer is still 'yes.' We are re-collecting the experience. The act and intent persists though the content might vary.

Does the notion of 'revisiting' an art object make them a kind of unique reticulated vessel? Meaning they catch and hold data, including your interactions, like a kind of network or web of stored information. Your specific information about the object. This in turn suggests a much easier way to think and remember. Why bother to sustain information, keep it eternally at the ready, if we can transfer it over and out from inside our own heads. And more importantly, if there is something to which we can refer if need be?

It's like the vampire counting the seeds over and over again. If it had invented the concept of numbers, it would just need one nice big one like 3,000 before it needed to fly off somewhere. Then it could go ahead and count other piles. One and done. But one and done doesn't cut it. The counting itself is the essence, an action strung of many identical little actions, a collection of 'revisits.'

Merlin W. Donald suggests this to be the case when discussing our earliest primitive notations, which some harken as art sputterings. He calls these 'Exographic media [that] have important properties that are absent in natural memory systems...' (Donald 2010:71–79).

These oft-called 'symbolic technologies' deposit human activities into a magic hat—something that stores, transfers thinking and actions, communicates this on a different platform to others and yourself, and encourages 'revision.' What Donald is really trying to say is that we have invented a physical presence from a nonphysical thought.

The truth is that anything we produce does the same thing. The degrees of efficiency having everything to do with intent, attention, and emotional involvement. Art is but one category of freestanding, notational recording, which also has many levels of effect, depending on the observer's state of mind. An articulated wooden hat display from the 19th-century is allowed to be a magnificent sculpture mostly because my intention is no longer diverted to purchasing the hat sitting on top. That hat has long ago disintegrated. But when I do consider it differently, it begins to perform like a written list of 'to-dos' that externalizes a strict procedure of mental referencing actions so that I needn't work too hard to keep it all in my head. It stands as an algorithm, a procedure of commands to explain how to think about a human 'head.'

Let's first consider a more obvious kind of 'to-do' list like my little house cleaning one. First make the bed then sweep the kitchen. Here are three ways I can externalize this and set it free to live on its own so I don't keep cycling it through my brain as we often do when trying to remember things like shopping lists or telephone numbers. First, I can invent a catchy tune to whistle or capriciously sing. I can draw pictures in a specific order or I can just write it down. If the tune isn't catchy, I'll forget it. If the drawing has no punch to it, I'll forget where I put it. Same thing for writing a list.

Though in all these efforts, I have drilled it into my brain many more times over than had I done nothing.

Now consider the viewing procedure set down in a really effective cat drawing. First regard the typical big eyes, then the furry ears. Of course, it's up to the 'artist' to hook my attention. Therein lies the craft and the talent.

But let's say it does hook my attention. Then in walks the real cat. I spot the eyes and notice the ears. The drawing helps set and confirm the mental rule. All's well.

Does 'revisiting' have to do with casting a more durable mental slot that slips a here and now event smoothly into an already settled idea? For example, if you see a tightlipped smile on a woman, do you 'see' the rest of her as a 'Mona Lisa' and gloss over the many dissimilarities staring you in the face? In which case you are clearly 'revisiting' the Mona Lisa by using it to mediate how you visualize an aspect of the world. Could it be then that this image has wormed its way into your visualizing history by intervening on how you interpret light waves, a world we all filter in our fashion by constantly pushing certain reset buttons?

Art *per se*, including all forms of decoration, performs a fundamental reset or 'revisit' function.' Some loosely call this a 'coalition.' Our neocortex requires this to populate expedient recognition 'search' triggers.

Scientific research plumbs the neural idiosyncrasies of the extra-striate cortex in the temporal and occipital lobes, where activity ignites when we attend to these things. Though the brain must likely be humming panoramically, across all cellular clusters, and my guess at levels too low to be picked up on our present state machinery. But how do we then convert this entrenched, neural shorthand into a physical, stable, and freestanding repository?

***

The obvious answer is that some of these media have more pervasive effect than others. These 'conversion devices' can be exposed for what they are, the cognitive repercussions and neural designs that operate in tandem with life history behaviors.

These are the behavioral changes and responses organized by the biological passages we all undergo as we age. A newborn babe does not respond to the acceptable proportions or configuration of a young adult male face the way a young adult female does. The former is entering the world and depending on a reliable nurturer, the other is looking for a reliable mate.

In which case, all of these 'media' manifest in visualization 'to-do' habits that necessarily expedite survival imperatives, albeit with different emphasis as we mature, and that this in turn is affected by the variable challenges of our environments. This might appear rather dry and non-humanistic since it flies in the face of so many layers of self-flattering exegesis about human glory and creativity. Consider how many words and years have agglomerated 'meaningfulness' around art or design, meaningfulness, which is in turn all valid though insufficient for explaining the root of this remarkably productive impulse.

The overall 'art' process is more of a sliding intensification of mediated decisions about all of these 'media' toward a specific end— to form a caricature or an extreme shorthand that expedites how we memorialize and emotionalize our environment.

Emotions

Often the 'emotional' dimension in research and investigation is excised from the picture when it is the very fulcrum of our normal responses. The truth is that 'emotion' enters all of our efforts to demystify the world. Someone did not just sit placidly, better still, indifferently, and fiddle with obsidian scratches on a rock 1.5 million or 70,000 years ago. Not possible. Picking up 'something' to try 'something new' is curious and exciting and intriguing. It can charge your emotional system with adrenaline. It can focus your attention with fascination and discovery. It is not just an act of boredom or random whimsy. The chain of operations that sustains, in this case trying to repeat a scratch or line in the small rock, becomes an act of exploration and demystification of your world.

But one scratch does not an image make. Many more are required. What sustains this?

Demystifying one's world does not mean tracking just our individual or group response to sky, trees, sand, and all objects attached; it also means validating emotional responsiveness among all living participants. Not just perceived sensations by animals and humans, but far more importantly our assumptions about the nontangible messaging between living species. Our emotions presume this. Our beliefs and the narratives reinforce these assumptions.

Suddenly, the proto-human who decides to make more than one scratch is setting up a dialogue with the object, a dialogue with himself, and a dialogue with the process itself. What happens is he is using the process as a bridge to align himself in form and substance with, say, a piece of ochre rock (in the case of Christopher Henshilwood's find at Blombos Cave, South Africa). It is projecting himself as an actor to a third party - the rock. It sounds very Woodstock-ey to say this, but it is true. The sensation of holding the rock allows him to begin to transfer cognitively to it. 'Working it' is the transformative medium, not merely grasping hold of it.

'Conversion devices' are concatenated, time-based actions and not one-off, standalone mechanisms. Artists are people who best elaborate this. But just look at musicians lift their chins, shoulders, sway. They believe they become the notes they play. Violinists and pianists being the best caricatures for this. Their faces are unique for the emotional contortions. Emphasis on 'believing they become.'

This sounds like a vast and utterly exhausting enterprise of investigation, but it really all hinges on our imitative nature, which makes bold assumptions. If we consider something else in our environment, we are focusing outward and over, and in so doing, momentarily suspend our notion of 'self' by projecting life and identity to 'it.'

Some would answer, 'Not so. We are just looking.' And my response is that in humans, 'just looking is not that simple or dull.' That object of attention, 'it,' becomes the dummy we intend to talk back to us in some manner or other, however fleeting. That whatever is 'answering' us or others is doing so because we pried or injected ourselves into their precinct in the first place. We pried by one means alone and that is by means of imitation.

Unfortunately, there is no word in the language good enough to explain exactly the kind of projecting mimicry we are addressing. We have emotive terms like commiserate or consider. Empathize. Understand. We have mimetic terms like impersonate. We have offshoots of mimetic behavioral terms like simulate, copy, mirror, parrot, pretend, incorporate, appropriate. Just as Henry Walter Bates in his 1862 article for the Linnaen Society could speak rather definitively about genetic mimesis in butterflies as an adaptive process, he could not explain the 'how' of it, just the 'why' of it. And in the same way, I cannot find one word to explain the 'how' of it either.

Let's address the 'why.'

***

In the 21st century, is there still the same 'why' imperative for us as for butterflies, that of escaping predators by imitating others? On the surface, it seems to be just the opposite. No westerner is running around in Burkas and Hijabs as a disguise. However, our tendency is not to cling to our local traditions more staunchly, but to imitate even more by copying international dress codes, facial standards and uni-cultural trends. That we do this so fanatically leads one to suspect that the same underlying motives might apply—that we mime to adapt and avoid predators.

But what predators could a teen possibly know or care about?

Teens in America are not avoiding Isis. They barely know who their president is. They are, however, 24/7 trying to head 'potential' bullies off at the pass and the awful feeling of being outcast from their survival or procreative group because of looking or being perceived as even the slightest bit different. The number of their social media 'followers' might be dismally low and others could see it. Their 'likes' might be miniscule. Others could post awful things. They could avoid one's pages entirely. It hurts. For humans, surviving depends on a sense of belonging. So they stage 'happy' photos to impress others. This is their form of fakery and of wearing an elk mask to infiltrate the herd. We obsess to adapt. And we obsess to copy.

The mother of all conversion devices

We are the earth-walking octopus. This mimetic attribute is our _modus operandi_ and directly supports our success on earth. It both inures and lures us to _try to_ read the nontangible messaging across the larger environmental stage on which we perform. This means the subtle messaging among the inanimate or all that is defined superficially as not possessing a beating heart nor the ability to move on its own.

Emphasis on 'try.' We intend this because of the quaint but exasperating habit we have of doubting our sensory acumen yet believing we have the means, make that the entitlement, of figuring it all out. Thus, we are all at once modest and arrogant. We are inconsequential yet almighty.

The only way we can do all this is by developing hyper-sensitivity to 'effects' and inventing equivalencies for them; that 'this is like that.' With the term 'like' being the mother of all converting devices since it expresses in one tiny idea that every sensory input converges with others, suppressing and altering perception so that the notion of 'certainty' is always a negotiable target.

Let's take it a step further. Vision converts sound inputs just as touch converts vision, etc. In each case, it sharpens our focus beyond the original input. When we hear something in the background, it remains ambient if we do not turn our vision into a sound-seeking device to identify the direction from which it came. Close your eyes if you don't believe me. Now eco-locate. Have someone move about and make noise. Your eyeballs cannot suppress their mission to swivel in their socket and locate the cause.

'Touch' further converts the impact of vision too. What you see in the distance cannot be touched. When you finally do touch it, the story has changed. It happens all the time. Take that blueish, greenish triangle in the distance that I decide should be labeled 'mountain.' Up close, it is a confusing, sweaty, exhausting enigma of trudging through brush and slipping around rocks. The hodgepodge of the new full-body inputting necessarily alters the picture. A child cannot learn to visualize about depth perception and texture unless he extends himself and touches the world.

We know this so deeply and immediately that we make adjustments for our perception issues with standardized equivalency precepts. Some would call this symbolism, but if you did call it that, all animals are highly symbolic too. A dog hears the music of someone's gate and 'knows' it is the embodiment of its master. It converts distant sounds into tight cognitive formats that function as expectations of imagery and emotional rewards.

Or consider the honeybee. A bee 'waggle dances' in the air, and by so doing, sketches an ephemeral map that converts the experience of flying time and direction to good flowers and homes, which then somehow lingers as an entity in the brains of conspecifics. In this latter case, the bee is 'publishing' the media as an abstract fact. They see a map.

Though we humans are really, really good at this same game, it begins with fits and starts and remains mildly troublesome even as we grow wiser. When it comes to isolating those 'equivalencies' by capturing them in a stable, freestanding form, it requires remarkable physical and cognitive conversions or transfers. Not the obvious intangible onto tangible like looking at a sunset that is a two-dimensional spread of reflective light quanta and then fixing it in paint or graphite shading, but the motivation for even attempting to do so in the first place—in other words, the 'impulse.'

Recursion

For most of us, the 'likeness' concept drives our determinations to even invent equivalencies in the first place. On what could a communication system be constructed for any living thing were recognition of mutual identity absent? For example, if we first must agree that the moon looks like a face, we must first take for granted that you and I are similar and think the same way. And this has to be well-founded long before it occurs to us to symbolize anything. One wonders if language in any form could exist without this dynamic recursive context—the belief that 'I am (like) you.'

Why do I call this the basic ironclad recursion? Because it is the single operating principle of consciousness, a simple yet perfect sentence that reverberates throughout our communicative and active lives. It is the framing clause for all creative passages such as a thought sentence or any media construction, in fact for all human operations. And it immediately branches out to become 'I am (like) that.'

This is the ever-rumbling, inner dialogue between perspectives; to consider 'that thing over there' in terms of 'me, over here.' In the extreme, it can torment. The term for this self-dialogue, 'soliloquia,' was coined by Saint Augustine around 386 A.D. (see 'Soliloquies' 1910). It was for him then, as it is for us now, a percussive, deterministic, omnipresent, and cognitive structure apart from which conscious humans cannot seem to operate (as suggested above, autism is a putative case in which the intellectual understanding might be there, but the technically unassisted and coordinated ability to express it is not; see Baron-Cohen 1995, Sacks 1995, Grandin 2013, and Giovanelli 2006).

That notion of a soliloquy, in which some version of the 'self' addresses another form of the self, is predicated on the active functioning and belief in a fully unified sentience where the commingling of intellect, emotion, and bodily feelings is summarized as a unity. This seems counterintuitive since there seems to be a necessary split of perspectives. But that's the point. You can't split an apple that isn't whole first.

The Fronto Insular and Anterior Insular and Anterior Cingulate Cortices are significant for this kind of perspective locomotion. Paradoxically, autists have a higher ratio of a specific kind of bipolar neuron called Von Economo Neurons or VENs to pyramidal cells - a remarkably symmetrical neuron recently identified as essential to this kind of gymnastics. In some studies, this was found in young children to be an increase of over 50%. An overgrowth to be sure in an area (FI-fronto insular cortex) known for the integration of self-ism in terms of emotions, intuitions and social skills.

32

In the autist brains, the cell somata (the stomach or really the body of the cell) and dendrites (the branches that receive the synaptic impulses) are atypical. The nucleus of the neuron tends to be swollen and the dendrites are longer and present like corkscrews. The common assessment of this difference suggests a heightened interoception or a heightened awareness of the body's behaviors and needs to the extent that an autist's concern or awareness of other's physical behaviors and therefore social signals are distracted and subjugated.

But it is a bit more complex than 'selfishness' per se. They begin with an acute awareness of the apple split and have to work extremely hard to reconstitute it. Spinning and flapping arms is their kinetic way to literally pull themselves together, even compressing themselves in a 'squeeze' machine as Temple Grandin likes to do.

Behaviorists and anthropologists have long suggested that this dialoguing back and forth in real-time activity defines the *modus operandi* of the human species. That is, that it is outwardly and socially predicated on someone's assumption that their actions be answered back by someone or something else. Sanity expects this reverberation, which is why solitary confinement dooms those who are unable to construct a facsimile for dialoguing.

Stepping that up a notch, the suggestion has been and continues to be borne out in most anthropology and material archaeology tracts (White 2006; Pryor 2008; Turner 2008; Goodall) - that exchanging valued resources is a unique bridge between like respondents. It creates 'high solidarity' among conspecifics, with one of the most significant results being positive emotions. And positive emotions, it has been recently discovered, tend to keep long-term memory readily available in the hippocampus rather than shipping it off for archiving in the neocortex.

As early as 1924, Marcel Mauss took this 'exchange' idea a step further or rather a few steps backward. He noted that it might not be the object transferred that is significant but the reciprocity itself that ignites the flow of positive emotions and binds the giver with the receiver.

> ...and increases the individual's commitment to others regardless of what is actually being exchanged...there appears to be a built-in proclivity for reciprocity among humans.... (Turner 2008:93)

Reciprocity and recursion are almost identical concepts. I'm trying not to be extreme here, but I hasten to say they are more than just *almost* identical concepts. Think about it. In language, recursion is often defined as a parenthetical elaboration of the main clause. It's like a biological clade, an offspring of the same ancestor. A recursion reciprocates the initial concept by restating it in some other way.

Adding a nose to a face is the same kind of thing. We 'get' the face part without the nose when there is just a circle containing two paired dots for eyes. We just add the nose to echo the main point—the face idea that depends far more on the eyes and mouth as the principal players in human communication. In any case, we are reciprocating facial assets. We don't really have to, but feel that to avoid confusion or to accelerate understanding, it certainly helps. Thus, we are also running back, *recurrere,* on the idea of face when we add another level of description.

Recursion is also implicit in the notion of dialogue, even self-dialogue, as in that wonderful word 'soliloquy.' A conversation with oneself.

> For many days I had been debating within myself many and diverse things, seeking constantly, and with anxiety, to find out my real self, my best good, and the evil to be avoided, when suddenly one - I know not, but eagerly strive to know, whether it were myself or another, within

me or without—said to me. (Book One, *The Soliloquies of Saint Augustine*, oll.libertyfund.org/titles/1153)

Philosophers can probably count on two hands the number of possible 'selves' implied in this work. Ironically, for me, the most obvious is the fact that he wrote it down. For whom? This action alone is a splitting or acknowledging of more than one self. The writer and the reader. It means he published it. Publishing is a formalized separation of oneself as shedding some form of a freestanding version of a person. It is a facsimile of that same person expressed by language that is stabilized on parchment. But it also reciprocates or runs back (recurrit) to the author as to who they are, what they consider themselves as being, and how they think. The list could go on and on.

It also attests to their underlying motivation. All writing is a reverberation or recursion, a long back and forth of parenthetical actions and descriptions. And this is despite having 'one thought'—as an editor on the New York Daily News once told me when I interned there, 'Just one thought,' he admonished and smiled.

Why is publishing so significant? Because by doing it, Saint Augustine, in this case, captures the many parts of his 'present self' in other media. He gifts it back to himself. He also predicates 'my real self' based on the similitude of others who might encounter the writing, including his future 'self' when he rereads it. It is a similitude that is a parenthetical description of the main clause - 'me.'

Think about it further. You do not offer a gift unless you assume what the receiver might feel. You temporarily invent yourself as this person. When it comes to verbal communication, you do not even open your mouth to speak unless you assume someone wants to hear you (hopefully). Quite naturally, the only basis for this assumption being yourself and how you imagine you would feel as recipient.

Every Little Movement Has a Meaning All Its Own

Reciprocity, dialoguing, projection of the self as the actor, all of these reinforce imitation thinking and form the basic emotional syntax that sensitizes us to the prosody of gesturing. Body language. For autists like Temple Grandin, she could not realize that people had subtle, expressive eye movements until she was fifty years old. She goes on to mention,

> ...it's not that autistics don't respond to eye contact, it's that their response is the opposite of neurotypicals.'
> (Grandin 2013:35)

The subtle use of muscles, even ocular muscles, is part of our expressive toolbox. We learn to respond by learning what the equations of these expressions are. This is why you have the lyric above from a 1910 musical called 'Madame Sherry.' My mother used to love singing it. I am certain it is a song that her mother sang to her, and one that my grandmother heard her own mother sing. It set the stage for attentiveness to prosody. The very sounds and tones that serve as vehicles for words but that have more meaning than the language itself.

All I know is that when my mother sang this song to me, she lifted her exquisitely sharp chin and ever so slightly waved her tapering fingertips. She was dancing while sitting, and we understood that she was visualizing herself gliding across the dance floor and all by way of the few little gestures she made. They were unequivocal.

How we come to understand this enormous lexicon of motions is fascinating itself. But the takeaway is that as newborns, we notice rather quickly what facial muscles work in tandem with others and which are specific to kinds of exchanges; which serve as prologue and indicators of specific actions and which do not. Later on, we learn how to predict based on this. We learn that the eyes of a giver light up just before a surprise gift—a good thing. Or adversely, how someone's eyes fail to respond accordingly from an emotional boost, etc. And this is a very strange thing.

There are neurons in our brains particularized for just this kind of sensitizing. Perhaps they are there not as a result of need like an expanding wallet, but just the opposite. They are there as normal tissue, and as a result, we use them as we do with our hands for touching. These neurons have so far been found only in large apes like gorillas and cetaceans, those seafaring mammals of highly communicative habits like dolphins and belugas. They are present in any mammal with a brain weighing over 300 grams, regardless of brain-to-body ratio. They predominate on the right hemisphere in the fronto interior cortex (FI), and curiously have the highest ratio in great apes, yes higher for them than for humans. Yet they are significant for sympathetic arousal, which is the first step to reading facial gestures. Their preponderance in great apes becomes less curious if you read descriptions of their social behaviors.

It quickly becomes apparent that watching and reading their leader's expressions is a fulltime job, and exquisitely *de rigueur* in their communities. It's a full court press all the time because unlike ourselves, they seem unable to codify body language and must remain ever vigilant. We predict by it whereas they fail to connect the dots. They live in the moment regarding social interactions. They never seem able to identify themselves comfortably in others. Therefore, they need those neurons to be ever vigilant, whereas we have invented a shorthand system called syntax.

Syntax does not belong to word arrangement alone. Let's take a look at my own or your little nuclear community. When I purposefully freeze my face during a conversation, my husband or children suddenly ask, 'What's wrong?' They assume I am angry with them merely because my face does not reflect their expectations of how my face should answer them. The highly specific structure we have built regarding expectation of gestures is disrupted because my syntax is off. My expressionless face does not agree with the context of the conversation. It is a bit shocking.

The emotional surges that shuttle these events through the brain from the entorhinal cortex (Brodmann 28 and 34) through to the short-term memory-maker in the hippocampus require hefty emotional glue to stick the event to a memory. Therefore, it is not surprising that the amygdala plays an enormous geographical role in this complex. A. J. Macdonald notes regarding his research that 'the results...indicate that the amygdala is one of the principal targets of the entorhinal cortex' (Macdonald 1997).

And no emotional event is one-dimensional. It is never simply, 'I gave him a present.' Almost immediately it becomes, 'I gave him a present and he was delighted.' Or, 'He didn't respond,' signifying conflict. Or, 'He didn't respond enough...' Or, 'He didn't respond as I had hoped.' And then all the little emotional and social ramifications cascade forth like feelings of being pissed, suspicious and hurt.

No, indeed. It is hardly simple and flat. Just the opposite. It is a full-fledged, cubic story with a highly reticulated narrative of multimodal inputting. Even many varying layers of neural oscillations that link or synchronize certain cells with each other by the wave patterns of their synapsing. In other words, the brain beats like a metronome. Not one metronome, but many metronomes.

The autonomic metronome is pulsing at a different rate from the thinking metronome. The inhibitory metronome affects the excitatory ones. And the oscillations in many cases can vary depending on the location of the cells. More interestingly, and this has been known a rather long time, these pulses can vary according to the emotional and attentional investment we have in an event.

Gamma waves, or a frequency band of 40 to 70 pulses per second, have been linked to cognitive processing. It is a directive issued forth, many say, from the thalamus to coordinate the brain in regular looping sweeps. It most effectively coordinates the action potentials. These lowest amplitude waves seem to be our cognitive sweet spot for neural binding or thought binding. Ironically, it is also the band width of flicker fusion for visualization coherence, as already mentioned. When light flicker falls to slower Beta pulses of around 30 Hz or fewer, we tend to see the oscillations of a computer or TV screen. At fewer than 24 frames per second, we see individual film frames, which cause the flicker sensation. It is very distracting, and this tends to confirm our neural safe zone for being the gamma frequencies.

Alpha bands are consistent with relaxed and fairly inattentive wakefulness. Factor in the release of adrenaline from emotional interplay and you are speeding up the thalamo-cortical synchrony of your brain for concentrating. Ironically, EEG's from meditative monks with a good degree of experience, show the highest degree of consistent gamma waves. Typically, we associate meditation as a hyper-relaxed state. The opposite of an emotional state.

But the kicker comes when the monk is asked to describe what he was focusing on when these waves drenched his brain. Because it is indeed an emotional state. One of compassion, where neural activity lights up the left pre-frontal cortex and not the amygdala, the worrying part of the brain.

Still, there is still a great deal we don't know about neural binding and emotion. It is now suspected that oscillations might have something to do with autistic behaviors. That the synchrony regulated by the thalamic pacemaker might be somehow off, irregular, or gating synapses in unusual patterns. At this juncture, it is irresistible to avoid suggesting something. That something is that 'compassion' begets a high degree of concentration and alertness. And compassion epitomizes empathy, projecting oneself as if we were the target of our attention. A robust Theory of Mindedness seems to be a gamma-wave enhancer.

And one sure way of learning the ropes of empathy is by means of our most reliable behavioral lexicon.

Twinkle, twinkle little star

The key we use to interpret this behavioral lexicon resides in the eye's pupil. Imagine something so complex becoming so decipherable a sign in so tiny a spot. If you've ever wondered about our optical focusing, wonder no longer. Humans are foveal creatures. We prefer to concentrate on pinpoints, moving pinpoints for certain and always, but itty-bitty dots nonetheless.

Generalized, nonspecific motion doesn't cut it for us other than as a useful warning to redirect our gaze. Part of that interpretation might be found in the brain's right temporoparietal junction (TPJ) which has been determined to be significant for direct gaze sensitivities. It is believed at this early stage in the research that this is a cognitive response to the 'story' concepts stated above, which involve mutually felt judgments. Judgments requiring the interpolation of 'self' as someone else and of putting yourself in their shoes to understand what they feel and what they mean to express. Typically, we find great comfort in direct gazes because we understand or think we understand the motives behind it.

It is therefore unsurprising that the autist brain should reflect the opposite since they find greater comfort in the averted gaze, and thus their TPJ inactivates or enervates accordingly. However, the left dorsolateral prefrontal cortex in most of us tracks our discomfort to the averted gaze, or expressionless face like mine was, a suspicious and uneasy feeling we get as a matter of course as we learn that these are signs of untrustworthiness, masked intentions, and our inability to penetrate or extrapolate mutuality.

A failed syntax. Imagine, there are parts of our brains that light up only when we cannot project ourselves successfully as the third party. 'Successfully' being the key word here.

But autists, whose wide-spectrum symptoms appear to share an inability to do just this, respond 'suspiciously' when the gaze is utterly direct. They take comfort in the averted gaze and get worried with the direct one.

At this point, it should be apparent that there is, nevertheless, an underlying self-referencing of some sort going on for autistic behaviors.

When you read some scientific data about fMRIs not lighting up in their TPJ or in other areas for lack of response to something, you might have to first put it in a more generalized framework. For example, many autists prefer to see the world from the corner of their eyes, in sidelong glances. Foveated seeing is painful for them, and for reasons that have yet to be fully determined. But the likelihood is that it is a combination of optical wiring in the retina and cognitive processing in more locations than we would naturally assume.

Science often assumes that an affinity for something is based on natural assets. You tend to gravitate to your natural assets. You become a great sprinter if you have particularly good muscle tone or high arches. But what if your assets are so overly abundant and your vision so naturally skewed for foveal or cone seeing that you are always trapped in the motion of tiny moving things from which you cannot disengage? Maybe you feel physically sick from it.

It's like a song you can't get out of your head and it's keeping you awake at night. Long ago, my thirteen-year-old sister wept her heart out and called for our mother to come help her. She couldn't get a Four Seasons song out of her head. It was '...driving me crazy.'

This sounds somewhat similar in effect as classic tunnel vision or Retinitis Pigmentosa. Often a degenerative and inherited disorder of the retina, it first presents with the loss of night vision, meaning the deterioration of low light rods so that all that remains is cone viewing as if in a tunnel. Most of our seeing occurs in the cone sensitive or daylight wavelengths. Should you lose nerve cells in the cone concentrated macula but retain rods, you are deemed officially blind.

Whereas the opposite is true with tunnel vision; you are not officially blind as long as the cones are functional. Autists certainly do perceive, perhaps just too much. They need the relief we normally get with every saccade and blink of our eyes. They could get a bit of a rest with a larger field of vision, greater scope and peripheral integration of information for every moment in their lives.

But could they handle all the extra information, the decisions, the distractions?

TMI

Thinking is a balancing act. It is always a question of degree about on what you wish to concentrate regardless of the intensity or length of time. It is a choice that comes easily for most of us. Whereas, too much of anything means that it is at the expense of other things, such as in a suppression or loss of inputs. Or confusion about what to choose or how to redirect thinking. This can be a disaster. It can sicken you.

For example, what if autists had a lower or much higher persistence of vision? Persistence of vision is the concept or theory that an image seen persists slightly in our short-term memories and is dislocated when a new one registers. The dislocation or impact of as little as two contrasting images flashing one up against the other, like stop and go signs, gives us the impression of motion. This illusion is called 'two stroke.' Or as some have suggested, it should really be called three-stroke for the following reason. This is best understood by the success of film and videography. But it is a cognitive construct.

The reason why some would prefer to call it three-stroke is that the residual of an image flash reverses its contrasting such that it can be construed as a second image in itself, though entirely neural—a negative mirror image of the initial one though it resides completely in our brain's mechanics. This then becomes the image against which the new image seems to flash up against (i.e., the third image). 'The contrast reversed neural image is then combined with the positive response to the following frame at the stage of motion detection to generate a motion signal' (Mather 2005:2016).

It is called two-stroke because there have really only been two inputs of light-generated images. The middle one is a corruption of the first. Thus, the implied activity of persistence of vision is in effect—that a sequence of flashing static images is construed as a unique motion. It might be the result of short-term memory behaviors that are inured to hold a flash of an image in our brain through the minute habits of blanking out periods like a saccade or a blink or more, until it is replaced by another light input. The juxtaposition itself or contrast then becomes the impression of motion.

Therefore, discordance is always converted in our minds to mean 'action.'

> [The] visual process involves a buffer storage which includes an erasure mechanism that is local in character and tends to erase stored information when new information is put in. Storage time appears to be of the order of one-quarter second; storage capacity is more difficult to assess. (Averbach and Coriell 1961)

Okay, then what if autists perceive very fast-moving things but at a slower clip than we do and still can't fuse a motion together as we commonly do? They see the fan blades turn as individual fins rather than a blur. Which we can do too. But it involves a huge commitment of brain time. We have to anticipate the pattern and in so doing predict the location and timing of the fins. This suggests that we intentionally 'erase' the short-term inputs faster than we normally do, and we do this through decision-making. Perhaps autists don't decide to do this but just naturally erase their short-term visual memories in far less than a quarter of a second. In which case, everything seems incredibly jarring.

Many high-functioning autists report precisely this feeling. A sensation of constantly segmented parts flying around. Consequently, they perform very badly at some kinds of visually tracking tests. Primarily because they have trouble tracking, they overcompensate and cannot welcome extraneous data from the peripheral field.

Or maybe the complete opposite. Maybe everything seems super-fluid and fused, meaning their short-term memories have a longer storage time. Either way, it is harder to dovetail compassionate thinking with neural binding (i.e., clear thinking) if any oscillation rates at any extreme exist. So, which is it for autists? Does it then follow that they prefer to fuse the world if only they could, or that they prefer a disjointed kind of seeing and favor distractions, anything to derail their monomania tracking?

Many autists have spoken of their aversion to frontal viewing, and of their desire to slow things, of seeing the world fragmented as in a slow-rolling film strip. They seem to want more time to digest the information streaming in. Separating specific motion by degree is placating for them. It is a fascinating concept in itself.

Most of us never think that movement is comprised of steps and is a linkage of tiny movements, where the brain convinces us that fragments necessarily become a smooth progress. But it is, and for many reasons, and not just for persistence of visual memory. For example, there is a natural oscillation of neuron synapsing in our brains, a clicking on and off of retinal neurons, of center on and off cells, of eye-blinking and saccade interruptions, of optic nerve blind spots, and the gated rate for light flicker mentioned above (among others).

Why do many autists like watching individual grains of sand falling? Not just because they can spot the minutiae faster *per se*, but perhaps because these tiny objects are separated and individualized frames of a large movement. Something they are used to. In other words, autists might be object-centric. I suggest that for a variety of neural reasons they are effectively tunnel vision-ed. Tracking motion is disturbing for them, off-putting and to be avoided.

At the same time, this is overkill. Too much focalized information. Too many objects, too much detail. Too little by way of suggestion at the cost of way too much definition that entraps one in moments. Normal functioning would stumble and falter if perceiving were constantly entrapped in moments. Being object-centric means to be trapped in moments. How could one possibly relax?

Eye contact and reading the prosody of intention in others would be extremely hard if you could not disengage from the object that is as specific as a set of someone else's pupils. You could not discriminate what other indicators are pointing to their intention and overall behaviors. You could not peripherally note their facial muscles, the cock of their heads, the shaping of their mouths, or even the gesturing of their hands. I think that not having all these facts of someone else's responsiveness to you and your actions would likely over emotionalize eye contact and tracking. For autists, it could be an annoyingly mysterious activity and a huge negative. Wouldn't you feel this way too?

***

These ancillary gestures cascade throughout the body and cause other subtle postures throughout. Body language or gestures are repercussions. They can be verbal and/or physical, but are always upsweeping composites, having intrinsic order to them. Long before I can spit out, 'I hate you,' the first indicators reside in and around my eyes, the shaping and aperture of my lids, the shape of my mouth, the tensing of my shoulders, how I plant my feet, and all well before I spit out the words. Almost immediately on birth, awareness of this streaming and recurring linked behavior helps us compose a reliable structure for the world.

And almost immediately on birth, our motor system and reaction motifs are set up for this natural rhythm of alternating observations with expected outcomes. We observe all kinds of connecting threads of little indicators, and then on very little we eventually manage to predict outcomes, whether an emotion is negative, a colorful word will erupt, or a body will fold exhausted into a chair. Lewis M. Nashner explains that this alternating rhythm begins with our sensory motor system.

> Rather than assuming a strategy which simply reacts to uncertainties within the environment after they occur, there are intrinsic processes within the organizational structure for movement control which are based upon assumptions about how the environment is structured. (Nashner:112)

We come to lump all of these specific observations in tight packets that predict behavior and clue us to outcomes. Here is where the notion of 'intention,' also defined by its twin 'anticipation,' makes its dynamic presence known. It conserves our intellectual and emotional energies by streamlining our abilities to triage the urgency of a dynamic environment regarding our own best interests. We can strategize those energies when best needed for thornier outcomes. These in turn create linguistic concepts that codify nuances into shorthand cues for reading body movements and gestures, and in a broader sense, for all temporal gestures of our material world.

The question we must ask is whether we can take Mauss's observations a step even further backward toward its origination. That being that gross action imitation such as freestanding image-making, among other created expressions, might have a neurological puppeteer pulling the strings, and that the reciprocity Mauss and Turner address might be cognitively derived rather than per-eminently and socially imposed.

Syntax

One curious finding from casts of hominid skull fragments compared alongside ours seems to bear a trajectory for right-brain enlargement in an area significant for the linguistic interpretation of tone, emotion, and rhythm. Although this is grossly oversimplified for lack of tissue, it is generally an area much ballyhooed as dominant for artistic creativity (Livingstone 2008; Leakey 1993), a point we shall debate in due course. Nevertheless, this fits nicely into the notion that hominids 'signed emotional reciprocity over shared items or hooted it (We still do with exclamations like 'Wow,' 'Oh!,' and 'Yahoo!').

This full body/sound-gesturing might certainly have built up sensitivities and contexts for prosody and speech that logically developed earlier than left-brain, verbal linguistics, that is if one wants to develop theories off a single skull fragment with the understanding that disproportionate lateralization from enlarged neural massing takes eons to evolve. This is likely an enormous leap of evolutionary faith (though possible).

Yet one thing is certain, signing and adverts are all contextualized by the mannerisms of the sender. This is a '*chaîne opératoire*' of rather formal procedures; straighten your back, lift up your chin, heave your chest forward, plant your feet, wave your arms, then let out sounds—or something like that. If this isn't syntax, then what is? Procedures that are held in common convey and convert information. If you have specific hand motions that are choreographed to sounds, you cannot mess with the sequencing. Otherwise it's gibberish. You don't say 'Ouch!' and wait a few beats before withdrawing your singed finger. It comes after.

Syntax is very tricky business, this notion of order for the purpose of effect. By the way, all animals find a way of doing the same things we do, of flagging importance and of trumpeting their finds and warnings regarding such things as food sources, caches, nests, mates, and danger. All of these notions in the animal world have a single unifying purpose and medium; they must be propelled over distance. And syntax mediates signaling between sender and recipient. Otherwise the elements of the signals would be lost in the wind and leaves.

You cannot even begin to articulate a concept without the motivation of reciprocity and exchange. The legibility of image-fabrication depends on the syntax a community has determined belongs especially to it. This is its culture. And syntax in any manifestation constitutes finite rules that can sustain an enormous variety of applications. Finite rules can mean that which is redundant and accepted behavior by more than one person. I can speak my own words embedded in quirky sound structures but it isn't a working language unless someone else agrees to the scheme that immediately returns us to the notion of 'sanity.

One good reason artists these days cannot create in a vacuum and are so hungry to 'show' their work devolves from this basic need to determine whether others 'get it.' They understand that all artists are idiosyncratic, their marks and colors and forms do not arise from a standardized QWERTY-like keyboard. They need to test to what degree theirs is decipherable by others.

Letters are graphic insignia that we use to convert remembered sounds because we deem it so and on and on regarding more complex configurations and grammar. This is no different whatsoever from other plastic conversions. If I attach a jagged line to a fluid curve without fixing a triangular shape at a certain distance from both, then no one could 'read' this. It would be gibberish. But someone knew enough 35,000 years ago, to add that triangular shape for emphasis as a conversion device for 'head' even though the silly line for the underbelly of the ox in question really wasn't that common a pairing. They managed to read it as we read it today only because we have agreed through generation after generation to continue doing so.

*

You could bring Mauss back into the argument and say that the legibility of these lexical graphics which we decide should transpose human sounds or animal effects is a reciprocal gift, the exchange of which across time and space is the really significant ingredient. We read the specific animal sounds implied by the image, their howls, their thunder hooves, their bodies snapping branches, even the shrieks and whispers of human participants pursuing them or being pursued by them. These are more than letters; they are full sentences and paragraphs. It was and still is a language even if the animals have long disappeared and we don't tend to hunt.

I can hear the objections, that we don't hunt this way anymore and those animals have long disappeared. True. But that isn't the core of the language. It is only the subject matter. The fact is that plastic materials have certainly evolved but human perception routines have not. For me, mimetic designs are far more limited than is verbalizing. Shrieks and horrors!

Many years of drawing and writing convinces me of this. There are only so many successful ratios for distancing the triangular shape from the rest of the animal form which is both a very annoying but incredibly mesmerizing aspect of creating art. Over the years, I have seen so much 'bad' drawing and so little 'good' drawing. The variations in a given leg by a hundred students in the same class can be fractional, yet they are enormous. Two students can get the incline the same but one is expert, the other is not. Analyzing the reason is what teachers try to do. 'Conviction' has a great deal to do with this.

But how do you convincingly translate a drawing from life even if you exaggerate whereas someone else does not exaggerate but the drawing fails to convince? The nuances and the syntax are incredibly complex. On the surface, there appear to be rather generous and indulgent rules of engagement for artists. But they are precise terms nonetheless.

Far be it for me to tell you what they are. It's more impossible in my mind than citing a neural map of the brain. Habit inures us to those terms which we are rigorously researching all the time. And this is most important; we seek these rules in a feedback loop. We are always testing them against our own methods of recognition and alertness. That loop is a measure of our consciously seeking the semantic habits of recognition at the same time as we reinvent them—all the time, in fact. Yet these 'fixed terms' occupy many in the scientific fields regarding our recognition routines, how they are laid into our cognition, if they can be altered or improved, and whether they are genetically predicated. There is a scientific predilection for 'keys,' those monolithic paradigms that anchor all recognition habits.

Paradigms

This is why you hear a lot about those underlying structural controls or universal criteria that should cut across cultural styles. Science is trying very hard to burrow beneath those styles to get to the cognitive kernels. There are a great many words developed by a great many good minds that have entered our vocabulary and mean pretty much the same thing.

In the 5th century BC, Democritus considered vision a form of atomic phantoms or eidola, from which we get the term 'idol.' He was a disciple of Leucippus, the earliest believer in particles or atoms. That those tiny, perfect specks of copies of the full object affect our sensations is how we get the term 'aesthetics.' And that effect on our sensations is known as an impression. But wait, there are far more who reinvent the same concept and with still more new names. Take Stephen Pinker who likes the word 'sprite,' as does Patrick Cavanagh (Pinker 2007; Cavanagh 2001). Then of course there is Stephen Dawkins (Dawkins 1976) whose memory kernel that gets (temporarily) passed along like a gene is called a 'meme.'

But there are other words like templates, paradigms, ideas, and something '*a priori*' (espoused by Plato down to Ernst Cassirer, among others). There are schemata, filters, icons, and on and on. All of which in one incarnation or other are 'replicators.' That is, they engender faithful, prolific, and long-lasting copies (Clayton 1997). This means they are the unembellished truism of a given category of object.

This means an icon or symbol as well, something by which all variety is controlled. With icons there is no need for large sub-sentences, riffs, or extraneous detail. But they are highly inadequate when discussing imitative behaviors because human cognition is far too sophisticated not to ignore or subvert these hackneyed mimetic devices. Is a typical apple always red and round?

I get so angry that I see red. Is this synesthesia, really?

Let's go back to the working notion that 'I am that' or that I could be 'that.' This concept explores the spatial distance between the 'self' in terms of a potential 'otherness.' It has wonderful implications of time concepts that result from this sense of the self-traversing between places; traveling across some concept of time and space to join in or elide with something else's behavior. Or really, the belief of just joining with the mere manifestation of a 'thing.'

Locating oneself anywhere involves hard work and the integration of 'modalities.' But it is impossible without some sensory cue overriding or calling the shots for others. This is called 'capture.' In humans, as already stated, it tends to be visual cues always over-lording it. It's just a matter of visual neurons and placement numerically superseding and outweighing any others. 'Visual capture' occurs when we trust or determine that sound sources originate where we decide them to be visually. Peter Battaglia explains this rather nicely.

> [In a] movie theater the visual information is located on the screen whereas the auditory information often comes from loudspeakers located to the side of the screen. Nevertheless, we perceive the sound to originate from the location of the visual stimulus (e.g., the moving lips of a face or the crash of an automobile). (Bataglia et al. 2003:1391)

This is about an integration of cues. And as with most aspects of our lives, there are degrees of this as there are with anything. In some cases, we strike a nicer balance between sensory cues, and at other times, there is a 'winner-takes-all' competition.

Scientists wonder, as they should, how we determine those nuances and what modality should lead. These are probabilities that have everything to do with an individual's personality makeup. Some cues have a lopsidedness to them based on a prior decision about content, and some we allow to be altered by additional facts and are thus posterior. Beliefs, habits, personal histories, memories, all of these and more skew the cues (much of this theorizing becomes highly mathematical around the theoretical ideas of Thomas Bayes during the first half of the 18th century, and later expounded by Pierre Simon Laplace during the second).

How the notion of 'capture' being any different than synesthesia in basic concept is debatable, at least for me. Though I grant that it is a more pronounced sensory swapping out. For example, the artist Wassily Kandinsky would have us believe he was a pure synethesiac meaning two sensations seem to be equally triggered by one stimulus. For him it was so valanced as to result in a highly symbolic structuring of the world through color and sound equations. Also, he was a theosophist, perhaps as a result of his neural wirings. Perhaps, not. I am hazarding a guess that religious symbolism layered over everything prejudiced his color sensitivities.

Nevertheless, if I am angry, I might see or project a red burst. Or I might just associate my anger with iconography that I invented or was invented for me. I might replace your face when you yell with a dragon's. In both cases, the sounds trigger a spontaneous and seemingly automatic visualization.

Again, this is a question of the integration of cues, of what modality I choose to overpower or capture others. Synesthesia suggests I do not choose but rather it is chosen for me by my neural idiosyncrasies. I am not sure. But I am certain that most scientists would disagree with the sub heading about seeing the color red. I challenged the classic notion about this condition on purpose. It's just that some folks ascribe color symbols systematically or aural signals to visual cues, while others' brains work differently. There is no instance when some sentiment, idea or sensation, does not overtake or capture others, or when sensations do not struggle to coalesce a unity.

Norman Doidge (2007) and others have done work framing this out for the blind, who must visualize by means of touch. Some of really fine work concerns those who are 'recently sighted' (Sinha 2006; Arnheim 1990; McCleod 2001) and must learn to entrust their former 'capture' routines to their newly optical functionality. Let's just make it simple and stick with the term 'generic synesthesia.'

In generic form, 'synesthesia' is a very significant mediating device, particularly for visual recognition. It allows us to conceptually posit ourselves into another vessel. Here we are switching up a visual impulse with other senses, not just imaginative and emotional, but a physical response felt in our muscles and joints. Even in our taste buds when we see someone eating a delicious meal.

I remember as a high school student visiting a museum with a friend and sitting down totally exhausted. I asked him, 'If you think about biting into a lemon, what happens?' He answered, 'My mouth waters and puckers up.' Sympathetic to be sure. And most would not call this true synesthesia either. Nevertheless, it is the neural interfacing of distinct imitative capacity during which we visualize 'feelings' or produce other sensations when we visualize. Without synesthesia there could be no freestanding human record.

*

Conversion begins with this sensational interchange. Many would not call it 'capture' as I do because they deem the former to be an automatic cross-wiring type of sensory processing rather than premeditative swapping. When you really get down to the finer points, what's the difference?

Scientists must understand this basic conversion especially, from the lucid viewpoint of artists who cannot perform their tasks without the completion of a unique visualization by means of other sensations. But not all artists possess this kind of intensity or, frankly, response system. A prominent neuroscientist at Harvard known for her work with David Hubel unfortunately used the interpretations of a decent enough human being with sadly little persuasive art skills and constructed theory based on his revelations.

As with all things, there are levels of skill, intelligence, and talent.

The stronger a synesthetic response to viewing, the more convincing the image created. Artistic conviction tends to address this interfacing of sensations where sound and shapes are felt in our muscles, where a feeling or shape can produce a definite color, where a color produces an emotion. If I wanted to tell a student to 'jazz it up,' he would likely not be adding any blue to the picture, nor soft shadings. There is a vast landscape between sensing and responding despite the seeming simultaneity of it. It never travels along a rigidly proscribed synaptic loop where one sensation activates a solitary sensory-motor stream. Hearing noise and making noise are not the same kettle of fish. Nor is imitating a noise you hear. 'Seeing' is an active response and is not a simple mirror reflection.

Receiving light quanta through the retina is not the same as visualizing. And our motor response to haptic sensations such as that of sharpness on my finger tip is highly interpretive. I don't know why scientists insist it is synesthesia if I see the number five every time I get pinched, whereas getting angry does not apply. It should. Because anger brings with it a whole host of visuals, memories, and graphics too. Emotion should qualify as the sixth sensation, but it just doesn't.

And we all don't equally retract our finger like an aplysia snail does its antennae when it has become sensitized (Kandel 2006) because my sensitization and level of alarm is not yours. Some, like my father, calmly held it in place to purposefully test for the sharpness of a knife. He might not have known the precise degree of pain, but his intention or superimposed outcome was paramount and overrode it. So does mine. My expectation of sharpness overrides the touch sensation. It is there even before flesh touches the metal. The scenario is fixed.

Which is why I emphasize 'intention' as a conversion device for imitation production. It is the notion of projecting an outcome or goal by means of a variety of sensory modes to a confined stream of information. Perhaps it is easier to describe this in terms of film editing, something I briefly did as a documentary filmmaker. Before you can select the unique frames, you need to decide what the scene is. Deciding what the scene is means determining where and how you 'enter' and exit it. This is a time bridge of very specific definition where you string together many effects to achieve your 'intention.' You decide beforehand what the visualization must be with details to be filled in.

My father loved sharpening knives far more than he liked using them. He directed his actions (i.e., testing a sharp edge) to imitate his anticipation or intention of what his scenario of sharpness should be until both dovetailed; the imagined prick with the real one. His anticipation was about imitating the memory of feeling that had remained with him—a short autobiographical story of which we all have billions. Even with our first baby breaths, we lay in tiny strings of autobiographic sensation histories that help focus our anticipations for causes and effects. With that comes what I call the 'cubic sensation of knowing.'

Visualization

This is not a discussion of 'representational' image-creating as with object imitation *per se*. Such an assumption has historically confused any reasonable exploration regarding the origins for our fabrication impulse (Faulstitch 2009, Smith 2009, Bednarik 1995). We must address all configured outputs, what we commonly call abstract too.

And while much of what we discuss applies to all somatosensory formats such as music, speech, acting, dance, etc., we'll let 'visual' anchor the arguments.

Ironically, the reasons for doing so become the best explanations for why humans itch to make manifest what they can visually access. Imagine the confusion if all our input pathways were equally stimulated for forming impressions. Thankfully, there is one sensory mode that tends to dominate all others. It is the one we genetically 'trust' more than the others. Just as a dog confirms its visual knowledge with its scent, we also have a final arbiter; if you hear a train coming, what do you do?

Visual dominance is rare among animals. Dogs trust their sense of smell. But our olfactory bulb is tiny and sits below our prefrontal cortex. Therefore, it is sub-cortical, and our only sense that has been so demoted as to bypass the thalamus. Here, layered neurons channel and sort already coded sensations for our other senses through the rest of the cortical and sub-cortical structures. For this reason, the olfactory bulb cannot compete with visualization processes. Nor can any of the others, when you consider that nearly half the brain (Purves 2008; Ings 2007) is devoted to mediating visualization.

But remember, visualization does not mean vision. The former is interpretive, the latter is mechanical (Livingstone 2008; Purves 2008). You can perceive lights but can't configure the shapes without recognition habits, and this is purely mental. Visualization does not require the retina to sort and contrast light quanta from open eyes. Trances, visions, dreams, daydreaming, death vision, hallucinations, and more are largely close-eyed or non-foveated. What *does* inform visualization? Does it depend on at least once having had optical vision? Yes, of course it does, at least in some sense.

During the 1960s, when trying to rehabilitate their father who was a stroke victim, George and Paul Bach y Rita discovered the plastic capability of visualization and operated under the notion of what constitutes 'enough' to visualize. I add that this notion of 'enough' is also the magical little secret of creative endeavor. It belongs to the previous discussion of visual syntax.

Those of us who practice capturing information in an entity that is freestanding and can be revisited over time never cease to be amazed at just how we depend on the reader's ability to tie disparate prompts and suggestions that are 'enough' for them to recognize the whole. Some work together, others do not.

Belief

Where does one draw the line between good-enough visualization and totally helpless? Belief systems are really cultural judgments. These certainly help by kicking visualization up a notch. They are systems based on intention or anticipation, anticipation being a less robust form of intention. And 'intention' could easily be called a belief.

Beliefs filter ways of conceptualizing seeing by training the mind to seek by means of assumptions about certain themes - the Maori favor curvilinear and labyrinthine as did the Celts, and as we do today with body tattoos and graffiti. Pre-Greeks favored geometric, as did pre-Columbian, who even though they delighted in labyrinthine design, managed to express even that in angular form. Both were builders in massive stone so it makes sense that they wanted to predispose seeing the world in these perpendicular terms. Seafarers who lived by waves and currents naturally wanted high-perception training for such things that were the foundation of their successes. In other words, freestanding design fabrication served a perceptualization demand—to streamline visualization by bumping up 'recognition' assumptions.

Let me put it more mundanely. When I have been working out drawings only in shades of grey, you can pretty much bet that I mask the world with a like filter. My belief about visualization is spearheaded by a values prejudice.

Commonly, we assume that 'imitation' means 'copying' as in mimicry or better still as in facsimile even though we know down deep that capturing likenesses rests on the concept of 'enough'—that we need just enough information to get the point. Some of us like autists are at a disadvantage about what constitutes the minimum. But for each of us, the concept of 'enough' for any visualization varies according to our history and moods.

This then suggests that there's a fine line between perception and handicap. And herein lies the fascination of how we decide what the terms of 'enough' might be. Because it seems to be driven by the clear and present nature of the 'task.' Paul Bach y Rita, the scientist and rehabilitative doctor, pointed out that perception is more about the goal and less about the nature of the information. I couldn't agree more. This is something we all instinctively know, so much so that we take it in stride to adjust our informational requirements throughout the day, and in a much broader sense, throughout the various stages of our lives. Except it is not instinctive; it is learned and becomes semantic.

***

A decisive catalyst is our desperation to survive, and more prosaically, our need to navigate amidst what clutters the three dimensions. Think of it in terms of a densely packed cube. Let's say we are a little ball embedded in the matrix of this very fibrous cube and are moving through it by virtue of the initial momentum of just being born. We are kicked forward and thereafter are off and literally running or rolling in this case. The 'clutter' is the fibrous material that envelops, combines with us, and counter-vales us in three physical spatial dimensions (i.e., width, depth and height). The little track we impose of our progress is from our disturbing these tightly packed fibers, but the time track can also be characterized by many little fibrous obstacles we have pushed aside along the way.

Our desperation is to not only survive amidst all this, but to just get to the next point. I remember as a child hearing the wisdom of the artist Louise Nevelson, who worked right up to her 88th year. Her explanation for longevity (as I recall it) seems to square with many other octo- and nonagenarians, 'Never stop moving.' But movement implies self-placement, navigating against and around fibrous clutter and against the ticking of time, which constitutes a string of constant choices. If the momentum of living is propulsive, our cognition has to work off some system that adjusts for the speed of our progression, which brings us back to the notion of 'enough.' But this doesn't make any sense. What does forward momentum have to do with minimal information?

A high-pitched noise against the din of Times Square in New York City is hardly as descriptive as the one you hear alone in the dark. When alone, less is more, and the notion of 'enough' as plain as day. Or consider that when you drive at night, you guide your car with a meager few lights scattered on the road, and the resolution of the middle white line incredibly devalued at best. But you manage because you have to; you altered the terms of how and what to anticipate and what constitutes enough information.

Or take your 'task' to pick out *my* child's face in a crowd. Your heightened sensitivity is not going to be the same as mine. I will make much more out of much less information than you will unless your task has a distinct emotional component such that you might lose your babysitting job if you mess up. Still, it can't approach my basket of enough information. 'Less' is worth more to me than you.

Or as I recall on 9/11, my recognition paradigms for my children became so highly eclipsed because I had very little time to pick them out from the smoke-filled basement in Brooklyn and rush them out. I worked off far less a configuration of information and chose some caricature of them that was significantly enough for the task. Maybe it was a configuration of the color of their sweater with that of their hair and my working memory for their height. Whatever it was, it was far less than normal that day above all others.

Imitation Absolutes

But it constitutes imitation thinking. As you can see, imitative absolutism is impossible by virtue of individuation, task, location, perspective, and the material interpolations by which we mediate them as in wood, plastic, metal, or bytes. This seems to be ludicrously obvious, but it needs to be addressed. There is no such thing as facsimile. Period. It is more like facsimili-tude, and we all know this. It is this deeply understood acceptance of recognition vagaries that compels us to constantly re-up improved versions and strive to 'get it right' over and over again.

One overarching precept for all conversion devices is a psychological motive; to get it right. But how do we know what 'right' is unless there is an *a priori* decision guiding it? All of our fabricated designs represent such attempts. What is significant is that for humans, it appears to be a dynamic response and not a static one. We need to reassess constantly what 'getting it right' is. But, why?

Well, it's not just for the reasons stated above, but in a deeper sense, it is consistent with the activity of our enormously prolific synaptic spiking or action potentials, which no matter who does the math, is difficult to definitively assess. This is because in a given second, some cells are more successful at connecting with another neuron and many are not. Nevertheless, it's enormous, sometimes put at as high as 10 to 20 quadrillion, give or a take a few tens of trillions, depending on your activity, whether a neuron fires a neurotransmitter and what kind of cell it is.

What all of this connectivity is in effect doing is constantly re-perceiving. Thus, perception is really re-perception. We continually practice re- perception because by applying the same old perceiving formulae, we are essentially blanking out just as we do when we foveate too long or forcibly stifle our saccadic impulses to jump around, whereby 'there is a rapid disappearance of stabilized images' (Purves et al. 2008:297).

*

Our visualization system is designed for novelty. It doesn't mean that we are alone in this gambit; other animals must do the same. But we go to great extremes by creating artifices to ease the pain of adjusting to novelty.

We have to do this because we mix things up by means of 'capture' (i.e., Transferring a set of attributes in one sensory stream such as optical by means of another such as touch. Ostrovsky 2006). For example, as I was 'looking for' my children, my fingers were like sensors anticipating and therefore 'seeing' them by their touch. I was projecting a cubic scenario even as I was sorting the light quanta into a premeditated decision about their identity. Consciously, I might not have been able to tell what specifically I was looking for. Unconsciously, the likelihood was a variety of artificial groupings by traits: hair contour with color, or height with eye-spacing.

But with the accelerant of fear, my re-perception was heightened. The likelihood being that certain neurons were alerted to speed their oscillation rates for spikes and my focus or general attention to ambient information being virtually shut down.

62

Had I forgotten my glasses, my paring of traits would have been altogether different. You might try watching a news program, for example, with your glasses off. The likelihood is that you'll recognize some people through this blur. This is remarkable nonetheless. The reason being that the feedback loops for human perception are highly versatile. They constantly manufacture new thresholds for recognition paradigms. In other words, they like variety, which is very good.

Scientists such as Bach y Rita suggest there is a reason for this versatility, contending that sensory inputs, no matter where they are distributed, transfer the same base coding of universal electrical bytes, an untapped versatility that is regularly rerouted to a number of sensory motor systems (Doidge 2007; Merzenich 1983) and can be artificially manipulated. He based this on his father's complete recovery from a stroke in 1959 that destroyed 90% of his brain stem, and a considerable portion of his cortical motor functions (though I remain doubtful of these findings given the means available for calibrating the extent of cellular damage).

When an autopsy was performed on his father six years later, the lesion was still there. This builds on Vernon Montcastle's discovery that most of our sensory cortex, or neocortex (i.e., audial, visual, and haptic), is striated into six neural layers that decipher primary sensory inputs before channeling them back to the thalamus (Hubel 1986). Bach y Rita couldn't see why these universal information bytes could not be used equally well in such similar cortical material despite the differences in their location (Doidge 2008).

In other words, a cell reacting to a universal brain code the same way no matter what part of the brain. Interestingly, this idea of his dovetails nicely with the invention of universal computer language for an IBM design, a time in 1956 when Werner Buchholz invented the term 'byte.' The likelihood is that Bach y Rita was aware of the versatility inherent in the IBM invention, and that applications could apply universally.

He was right. But only to an extent. Even now, we still haven't got a handle on the coding of neurons, the base language they use to transfer data. But as a result of his own theory, he invented a fair number of transformative sensing (rehabilitative) machinery. Beginning with 'vibrating stimulators' attached to the dermis of a congenitally blind woman's back, he attached them to the electrical impulses of light levels received by a camera. To her, it was 'seeing.' An imitation or map of something coalesced into visualization.

Despite all this, controversy persists about just how plastic versus just how cyto-architectonic (i.e., locally specific variations) the neo and extrastriate cortices are. As with all things, extremes make any argumentation almost silly. For example, there is no question that Gabrielle Giffords, whose language functions were damaged by a bullet, still struggles with language execution even though she understands it. She can sing fine which suggests that the Wernicke functions, the rote formations of sounds as words is more intact than her Broca's area which centralizes the conceptual production of language.

Time will determine how fluidly convertible these functions become for her. The general architecture of our brain is demonstrated by these immediate deficits. Neurons have different shapes in different locations, different axon lengths, different tendencies to grow out dendrites, different levels of population within the various strata, and different connective preferences. They even have different 'flavors' for connecting vertically or horizontally.

For example, it takes on average 4 to 7 (though it can be as high as 20) color-sensing receptors in our eyes called cones to connect with a unique ganglion cell through a single bridge cell called a bipolar cell. And then with its enormously long axons, the ganglion cell becomes the optic nerve itself and finally the cross-shape channel called the 'chiasm' to further deep brain functions. However, the luminance or light level receptors called rods do not have that luxury. They have bipolar cells that converge anywhere from 50 to 100 other rods through horizontal links like strap hinges. It is by this means of summation that input is made with the ganglion cell, coupled with the inputs of much fewer cones. Vision has more to do with the way cells are wired than the numerical ratios.

There are approximately 18 varieties of ganglions, some of which allow a single, unique cone to connect to a unique bipolar cell and then to a unique ganglion at a ratio of 1:1:1. This intense acuity is called invagination, where a midget, bipolar cellar, obviously the very smallest variety of this type of cell, has dendrites that penetrate the pedicle of a single cone. A pedicle is the synaptic output end of a cone to its intended horizontal and bipolar cells. The same synaptic end of a rod is a spherule. Within that cyto-architectural determinism, which harkens to the original phrenologists that certain cells or parts of the brain do unique things, the dialogue remains heated, and for good reason. The challenge comes from the general fact that switching between sensory receptors is plastic and doable, that tuning some up while others might have withered is always at play.

But what about converting these interior impressions into motor behavior that executes that imagery? Where do these impulses nest and are they specific to cellular idiosyncrasies and locations? Well, that so-called conversion 'behavior' is incredibly clumsy despite our having done it since time immemorial. Add to that the genetic constraints and assets of our species, that our ability to visualize imagery is certainly not that of a barnacle nor hawk.

*

Genetics: That which is 'Enough'

Einstein noted: Everybody is a genius. But if you judge a fish by its ability to climb a tree it will live its whole life believing it is stupid.

For example, we are mere tri-chromates in comparison to some insects and fish that are tetra-chromates (e.g., honey bees, butterflies, most birds like zebra finches, but also zebra fish, etc.). Their color spectrum extends into the fourth light spectrum of ultraviolet (Hauber 2010). I could no sooner depict what visual cues are 'enough' for them to spot food because I can't even receive quanta on the same wavelengths. There's just no photo-opsin for that wavelength in my retinal cones.

But many nocturnal animals like rodents (e.g., rats, mice, gerbils, and the South American degu, a cousin of the guinea pig) do have these opsin proteins and can use their ultraviolet vision to track the urine of animals, perhaps even the gender (Dugatkin 2010, Hauber 2010, Curtis, Ings 2007, Pickrell 2003). I am certain that those seeking the elusive Sasquatch wish they could do the same during their nocturnal stakeouts.

Some animals like frogs 'see' a single photon, whereas our light-sensitive rods, though reactive to a single photon, are sluggish in their registering of this and sluggish in their ability to regenerate the rhodopsin pigment that would otherwise allow them to react to new incoming quanta. They can't efficiently get the signal through the optic nerve because they do a group-think or summation with other rods sometimes in the thousands but must share it all with a single ganglion cell. Though very indirectly and hardly at the streamlined ratio of those luckier cones. Imagine how 'nuts' we'd be if we could be distracted by a single photon. We'd all be begging for induced night vision to stop the madness.

Scotopic or night-vision animals obviously can't depend on color so much as they need to depend on low light (Purves 2008; Ings 2007). We also depend on low luminance distractions in our peripheral visual field for global or ambient vision to take the heat off the cones so they can recharge their cells, which they do at a rate that is four times faster than the rods. Global vision gives us a chance to decide where we want to concentrate looking, which is a job belonging to cones. It gives us a purview of what matters being looked at and affords a sense of penetrating depth and implied motion that tunnel vision or non-rod vision cannot.

Individual experience fine tunes skills in anticipating outcomes and heightens our perception even within the constraints of genetic coding. What I deem is 'enough' information to visualize a face or a running deer or a flip book is not the same as it is for cats, nor is it even the same as it is for you. Art or image-designing is a training precept that conditions us for what is enough information to catalyze recognition. This is an autobiographic and sequential buildup of experiences, and an acuity that is fluid, faulty, and fleeting.

Although certain optical mechanics appear to be automatic. One of them is called 'Persistence of Vision,' which fuses individual frames or flashing elements into an impression of motion. It is done in much the same way as we fill in the blanks from saccades and from the blind spot caused by the optic nerve egress from the retina. In this case, by erasing the dark spots between the changes. If we noted the lapse or dark interval between two frames of film, it would throw off our intention of seeing. But the eye clings to the previous image for an additional 40 milliseconds, thus allowing the image to persist in the retina until replaced by the next one.

Whereas the *phi* phenomenon is the brain's ability to insist that contiguous changes, either in a unique object flashing in a sequence like dots lighting and fading one by one, or one object fading against the flash of a different one, intends motion. For those who have edited film or video, the *phi* phenomenon can be disrupted because we are trained to see faster. And by that I mean anticipate changes. It comes from expecting the iteration of an image with minute changes. But it is still a sequence.

One must then wonder whether there is a mechanical exercise instilled by art. In its most essential use, it can acclimate us to the familiarity of objects to such a point that we can slow the *phi* phenomenon. Great familiarity with something, in any format like repeatedly drawing or carving fish and in other formats like storytelling and beliefs fertilizes synapses by extending the breadth of their reach and the complexity of the connections by virtue of the variety of ways we are taught to consider the object. If this pervasive kind of describing did not dominate thinking for, let's say, the Bare and Manau Indians of the Amazon's Rio Negro in Brazil, they couldn't have done what Richard Spruce describes of his specimen collecting in 1851.

> The archer stands motionless in a canoe, sees a fish below the surface of the black water, instantly calculates the angle of refraction and speed of swimming, releases his arrow just hard enough to hit the fish... '[or surprises] the birds still asleep in the trees when I could no more discern them than I could the fish in the waters.' (Hemming:185)

Hunting, tracking, all these basic survival skills are man's effective disrupting of the *phi* phenomenon and very likely the rejiggering of the persistence of their mechanical vision. That we populate our world with so much imagery iteration certainly suggests to me that we need the constant subliminal support for stimulating our lazy and lapsing perception habits. Hardcore survival routines demand we stay sharp.

Mimesis includes abstractions

Representation or mimesis of something in the form of an identifiable object does not adequately address the impulse behind all these fabrications. We rightly have to include in this mimesis discussion the profusion of manmade abstractions that appear to be just lines, forms and colors (Livingstone 2008; Hubel 1986). Such elements might be specific to our genetics rather than being some kind of esoteric creative effort. I'm being very nice here when it comes to florid explanations of 'abstract art,' which can wax prolific, grandiose, turgid and frankly damn annoying. But you certainly *can* speak of colors and motion and the implication of emotions from it. And there is good reason for being able to do so.

If imitation is the compulsion behind such things, it becomes obvious that these 'strokes' are merely isolated examples of human neocortical processing machinery presented on a stage as singular performers to drive home the means by which all human visualization is rooted and therefore perceived. They are the literal building-blocks for human vision. Isolating them and enlarging them a billion-fold is a good thing. A smart thing, in fact.

Abstract art performs a necessary task by focusing front and center on the neural media we employ to invest recognition both for objects and effects. It can be as simple as a canvas, let's say, divided into three horizontal segments. The lowest strip is something darkish. The top and largest strip is a bit lighter. And the third horizontal strip is a skinny edge separating the two that is lighter still than the other two. When you see this, you are visualizing the contrast prompts for twilight when the sun is just below the horizon.

But how many of us are keenly aware of this as a standalone fact that to humans, twilight casts light around the edge of the object (or horizon when viewing a vista) and darkens higher up in the sky? You may think this is pure invention when I say it. But when you are in Paris (book a trip, what the heck), try standing on one of the bridges at dusk and see what happens to the light in the sky just before it slips the building contours into obscurity. If not Paris, which is a very nice place to see this phenomenon, it works just fine anywhere else on earth.

Keenly aware? No, most of us are not. But subconsciously aware? Absolutely. The fact is that we 'know' this formula deep down in our semantic knowledge that this is a macro-formation of bold striping that has emotive resonance as day breaks or descends. These are times of the day when our anxiety and emotional levels naturally rise. Maybe Mark Rothko was trying to elicit these neural responses without really knowing he was angling for a primal prompt.

It's like the notion of ululation in ethnography, a horrible sound repeated endlessly and usually in a mourning context. Here, (usually two) articulated decibels take center stage, laying bare the basic structure of language as an emotional expression in its most guttural simplicity.

Abstractions in this extreme, be it decibels or shapes, are not pure abstractions. The appellation is unfair. Abstractions should be considered as those 'enough' elements that reveal the signature biology of how our species registers inputs and, therefore, outputs.

For example, if our primary visual system, located in a hub of neurons in the (occipital lobe) rear of our brain, is in part constructed of neural columns and 'blobs' (Miller 1987) that can only restrictively sort light information from the optic nerve as linear angles, then is it so farfetched that we are somehow compelled, if not utterly confined, to consciously inculcate linearity since it is the crux of our visualization alphabet?

Writ large, they seem to be the codes by which we humans mentally sort light information, and it is likely not the way a fish does, nor any other species for that matter. Exposing ourselves over and over to the terms and limitations of our sensory filters is just smart business. So, thank you, Piet Mondrian, Arshile Gorky, and Wassily Kandinsky.

**

If we cognitize vision inputs by means of a neural angle grid, why not just make consciously manifest what those angles (lines) sensitivities are? Imitate them big, bold, and large. And thank you, Franz Kline, too.

Taken a step further, could it be that these abstract marks constitute our best efforts to practice 'seeing' rigorously? All of which, I suggest, is intentional or rather 'purposeful' as in basic functioning within your natural environment. Those 'abstract' marks accurately replicate how we 'transpose' vision into visualization. They become didactic simply because they help us practice doing it.

Biologically, they are also incredibly accurate and revealing. If we have always used lines angled this way and that way as our earliest and basic plastic grammar implies, (Stephen Henshilwood has found what is believed to be an intentionally cross-hatched piece of iron ore dating back 75,000 years in Blombos Cave, South Africa.), then how could that not have been taken as the big clue to the deeper fundamentals of how we see? Even your toddler's first marks are the same zigs and zags.

Still more than meets the eye

Then come their curlicues. A fully enclosed circle coming later is taught and only successful when it gains emotional momentum by being an emblem for parents as represented for their faces. The physical making of a full circle is difficult to control and manifest. Therefore, one should suspect it's not particularly compatible to our neural preferences. Though, here again I wonder. However, the prevalence across all prehistoric cultures for spirals and such suggests that curved lines might be part of our visual-cortical matrix as well. Perhaps even the entire vortical form.

If these are in part automatic images, where and when have they been mediated so we can at least partially 'see' them in their purest form? The answer is we see them as phosphenes in our daily lives without conscious awareness for them being our basic design resource.

Phosphenes burst on to the scientific scene in 1816 with Alessandro Volta's experiments with extra cranial electric jolts. They were more extensively researched by Jan E. Purkinje in his doctoral dissertation of 1819 and can best be described as luminous, closed-eyed, optical effects that have nothing to do with our memories. They are involuntary responses. There is a menu of about 12 designs for each of us that is generally shared by all and can be instigated by just squeezing or pressing down on our eyelids. Hallucinogens and many other means can cause them. Yet the exact chain for them remains a mystery.

'Seeing' them has tended to be an 'enchanted' attribute of those in power like shamans, who often have access to drugs and whose demonstration of these annuli (rings) and other patterns are incorporated into sacred ceremonials. These in turn become icons of great 'meaning.' And it is virtually impossible when studying Paleolithic and especially Mesolithic iconography not to consider the implication of these phenomena. Yet, they belong to all of us.

Children are extremely capable and conversant with these circles and geometric shapes, including 'stars before your eyes' as everyone well knows who has every cried, sneezed, or rubbed their eyes. These self-illuminated optics or entoptics occur without the input of light. In fact, the entire lexicon of graphic shape elements we employ can be induced at whim just by putting direct pressure on the eyeball.

Dr. Gerald Oster did extensive work on this. And before him, Max Knoll in Munich induced a wide range of non-light-generated optical shapes that many anthropologists like James David Lewis-Williams decades ago and Robert G. Bednarik determined were a shaman's standard trance repertoire universally employed in rock art and the earliest cave art. But they are our basic and universal drafting palette. Instead of mixing ten to twelve colors on your palette, you mix ten to twelve basic shapes.

Take the sigma curve or reverse swirl 'S.' It is so pervasive a component of our graphic grammar and contra-postal structural applications that applying the same argument suggests that our brains feel extremely comfortable with this rather curved form of the ubiquitous zig/zag. Count both as part of our phosphenic palette. Accordingly, this suggests that further research might reveal a little more neural subtlety to those Hubel/Weissel rigid angle filters. I bet there are some robust curves and 'S' shapes in there too. In other words, the preponderance of curves and swirls in our imitation lexicon suggests that our visual cortex has a keen predilection for insinuating them.

The next time when you invest your attention in an enormous Franz Kline or Motherwell or Pollack, understand that you might merely be zooming in on the smaller strokes we use to process imagery. We are line creatures more than we are color creatures. The splatters of Pollack colors are not perceived as such. We track them across and around the canvas as lines, just as we do with a complex wall of graffiti. It is an attention time sync, where our manic love of following lines synchronizes us with the flow as it must have been for the manufacturer of the object.

The lines are a mimeograph of his physical effort. We are always drawn to understanding how others did or do it, what the origins of their motion was, and what the follow-through was. We seek the Hansel and Gretel trail of their crumbs. In everything, in fact. And it's especially true in art. Pollack's splatter are his crumbs, as far as we are concerned, that he moved from here to there in a linear motion to just apply the stuff. And we mimic him when piecing together the tracks of his motion. This too becomes a cognitive trap based on the way our visual system organizes data.

*

We are contour/shape creatures more than we are gradation creatures. We must be careful not to be lulled into thinking that 'color field' art is as docile and harmless as you might guess. Here, our instinct is fully engaged to disambiguate and to establish the borders.

We can't tolerate ambiguity so we seek out separations, boundaries and borders at all costs. Our eyes contain a mosaic of cells sensitive to neurotransmitters or chemicals that either excite or inhibit light processing. The effect is the notion of contrast. So naturally we find comfort in distinctions, in edges, in boundaries and of course in lines. Our genetics determine this routine to always seek these. Therefore, color fields can be a form of annoyance, mild perhaps, because we don't stay with it long, but annoying nonetheless. Eavesdropping on gallery goers reveals comments like, "What am I supposed to see?"

Two lights

A lot of this built-in contrast instinct is reinforced from our deeply embedded responses for the twilight hours in our daily lives. If the gentle contours, changes, and contrasts are too vague, we tend to ignore the view entirely. It is our nature. We are contour creatures more than we are nuance creatures.

And when we generate most intellectual interest in understanding our environment, it Is at a time when we are innately

74

detecting disconformity. The irony for doing so exists when conformity appears to be paramount. We understand inconsistencies and gravitate to them. Having found them we excuse them and move on. Aspects of this habit become obvious when quickly scanning a repeat linear motif like a sloppy meander register. Humans are very catholic at accepting anomalies in color fields. In fact, no one believes in the absolute consistency of any given mass of color just as no one ever sees it in the real world, mottled as it is by the interplay of shadows, light waves, etc. Even your bright computer screen does not appear wholly white. We know this semantically that it yields pervasive little, perfectly regular, contrasting clumps of greyish globs against bright globs across the field. We just ignore the mottled effect and overlay a verbal concept called 'white.'

Sensation is far more intelligent than words allow us to be, though we call it 'white' when it is hardly that. What we are seeing is the Stroop effect of the concept 'white' because the word tells us so. Whereas there are really tiny, contrasting brightness packets that express our retinal pattern responding to the equally proportionate distribution of on-center ganglion cells and off-center ganglion cells. That is, for a given level of luminosity,' center-on' or 'target on' cells fire action potentials with the light as a target found. For the others that are 'off-center,' the light is aberrant and shuts down the information.

I find it extremely disconcerting seeing these minute gray and bright spots across the bright computer screen. But there is nothing I can do about this. So, we accept ambiguity in color fields and seek resolution and distraction in lines. We quickly scan registers like meanders to determine if there is consistency or broken patterns.

One would be surprised how swiftly we decide that there is no break in the pattern or whether it ends up being no reliable pattern at all. Our preference is to believe it is regular and this too results from a behavioral directive that something benign constitutes a repetition whereas something worrisome is a unique break in a pattern.

If I could biologically access a process that does not favor linear superiority over color field, please introduce me to it. But this seems to be the limit of my genetic capabilities. Over and over and over we go with the same old same old despite our impressive digital/tech world. The perception formats remain the same despite the icons, bytes, voxels (cubic pixels), and pulsating screens. We are mesmerized by lines.

Conversion Devices

PART TWO

'I am that.' (again).

If you are at least a bit more receptive to the notion that visualization has built-in physiological limitations about which no level of human imagining and creativity can override, why not at least approach the subject of mimetic replication behavior in the same vein?

Modestly stated, it is an activity best described as infinitely describing ways to access the world but with distinct limitations; that there is an infinity of combinations to coordinate the effective inputs, but a finite smorgasbord of media to organize them. It's as if our species requires the extra cognitive boost through these manmade creative abstractions, be they abstract or representational, to convert a cacophony of linear and color sensations into a discrete thread of here and now.

This requires constant affirmation of decisions about phrasing and salience, about what to clump together for emphasis and what is boringly redundant, superfluous, annoying, and distracting. Wait, hold it a sec! We are getting too far ahead of ourselves. How can you clump anything together if you have no basket to put it? How do you gather petals if you have no hands cupped for holding them? How do you string a sentence together that is a timed sequence if you have no concept of navigating yourself from here to there? How do you understand effects if you have no understanding of what an instigator is - a cause - or how water ripples out in concentric circles if you never supposed a pebble to have been cast?

The answer is that you simply cannot. What we are talking about is not just a method by which to probe the world, but a strategy to hold it together. Where does this strategy gain momentum, let alone assemble?

***

The following is a brief discussion of a woman whose revelations have been largely contested. But we use it as a parable so to speak of how perception depends on strategies or the task at hand. It's an interesting hypothesis.

Barbara Arrowsmith Young ran a private school in Toronto, Canada for the learning disabled. According to Barbara Arrowsmith Young, she has stated that she had a malfunctioning Brodmann 44, part of Broca's area known to mediate verbal language. She maintains that she could not construct imaginary and therefore imitative premotor behaviors before executing her movements. I include a discussion of her self-proclaimed (and often questioned) deficits merely because it suggests the likelihood that others experience this and that issues she has brought up are germane to this discussion.

Unsurprisingly, Broca's area has been found to also be a hub consistent for imitative, premotor behaviors, where we anticipate the action of touching before doing it.

For Arrowsmith Young, this means she lacked a strategy. To anticipate is to strategize. It means you have seen that 'film' before and know how it ends. Apparently, Barbara Young had never seen that film before, or having seen it, never could remember it. Perhaps her remote-control camera was missing—that steady, singular, and reliable self-recognition that points us through time and space. It is a remote-control camera by which we automatically 'see' ourselves from a different point of view.

All of this depends on the functionality of mapping. That you are 'here' and either want to *get* or want to *be* 'there.' We become aerialists to a certain extent. Let's mark 'Here' with an 'x.' Let's mark 'There' with a '0.' From the perspective of the '0,' you can determine how far it is and which route to take back to 'x' or the physical 'me.' There is a second, more fluid scenario in which we can dismiss the 'x' location and simply postulate what the surroundings of '0' might be because we become that point in mental space and time. Autists simply cannot do this second version. Normally we are glib at this; it is as natural to us as regarding a mother's smile coming right back at us.

Temple Grandin, a very high-performing autist, describes a test that Maria Kozhevnikov (recently of Harvard) designed to filter these handicaps.

> ...this test required me to imagine myself hovering above the scene and see the angles from the perspective of a person standing below. Let me tell you, that's not the same as standing on the ground and looking out of my own two eyes...I scored a zero. (Grandin 2013:163)

Arrowsmith Young was not labelled autistic. She avoided the pigeonholing. Today, she might be. So how did all her experiencing and concomitant anticipation get garbled and lost? One reason might be that she or others like her had no key to switch on the record button. That key being a full-bodied and somo-aesthetic sense of herself as an icon, a unique moveable presence like a little ghostly chessman that could cross the great divide from an interior nebula of random feelings to an applied imagination of her own identity. By 'applied' I mean purposeful, working, goal-oriented, and therefore temporal.

Goals are temporal destinations and absolutely sequential. We move along our space time axis like a Ponzi scheme, planning the next goal even before we complete the former. We keep 'forwarding' the marker. She lacked an ego icon by which she could bridge space and forward the marker, and thus lacked a sense of continuity.

What are the attributes of this so-called marker?

It is something that allows us to stabilize the world we occupy and that we believe to exist by centering its gravity, so to speak, in terms of ourselves as what I would best describe as a moving vortex rather than the mythological and traditionally static idea of an umbilicus, fulcrum, pole, etc. In other words a mini me is the real umbilicus of each of our universes. And there is nothing new about that.

Vortices are dynamic and multidimensional centers with incredible centripetal forces. So are we. We coalesce sensations, which is a dynamic force, by sucking up everything in the moment as we move along. But we are not greedy vortices, but rather modest ones. Just visitors, really for a segue of moments. For to enforce stability or 'structure' on the environment and to 'read it,' we carry over this somatosensory routine by swapping our visual goal with this dynamic, vortical sense of self. And then we move on.

All our truly emotional words are based on this reciprocity, words like compassion or empathy or understanding or sympathy or trust. In the *'Lost Battles'* by Jonathan Jones (2012:63), he describes why Michelangelo had such an impact with his 'Pieta,' certainly a dramatic scene in itself. But it was so much the more heightened by this artist.

> The effect is absolutely to exact pity; to wrench out compassion. But this is because Michelangelo arouses the imagination. He does not portray a dead man with cool precision...it is an ordeal of the imagination. The emotional power lies in the eerie, relaxed clarity with which the artist shows himself what it would be like to be dead; to be the man in Mary's arms. *It hits, pricks you...a fact*

Michaelangelo has made himself know from the inside.
(My italics)

Arrowsmith Young described her reality as living in '…a fog, and the world no more solid than cotton candy' (Doidge 2007:34). She couldn't understand spatial relativity and it followed that she couldn't understand recursive or parenthetical relationships expressed in language as in the difference between 'mother's daughter or daughter's mother,' all because she couldn't press that essential record button that activated a reliable self-icon. She lived in a world that lacked separations, that lacked linearity, security, and reliability. How could she if there was no stable, reliable, vibrational referencing or pointing device… that being herself?

Why so many lines in our lives?

Lines are spatial barriers that are cognitized, and not just because of the neurons in our primary visual system. Margaret Livingstone noted the same.

> …we find line drawings to be acceptable representations of reality, despite the fact that reality contains no such lines…. (Livingstone 2008).

Well, it goes against my nature to say 'never,' and as an artist, these concepts are my stock in trade. But it is true to an extent because if I think of linearity in terms of connected little moments or dots as is the construction of any line, of course 'it' does not exist in nature as an entity but rather *de rigueur* as a construction. Though it certainly seems that drawing a line is a fluid, full-bodied, and unique action and with a unique tracery. It is accomplished by anticipating an unbroken flow. Therefore, it is cognitized. So, a process such as making a line hardly means that thinking in these terms or the *fait accompli* of lines is invalid.

Normal people don't operate in the world of diffusion and segmented thinking like many autists. No, we are the narrative animal par excellence, the stringer of lines from a beginning to an end point and positer of outcomes. So, from my perspective, 'lines' are real and good enough for me. They exist because I think they do. I project them.

Therefore, what needs to be stated is that lines are an essential habit of ours to transpose perception modes by means that presume physical boundaries. I consider them to be 'real' by virtue of the fact that this amiable media device is for us humans a great, great meta-tool. Lines allow us to complete something and move on. It allows us to process time and progress. It allows us to iconize ourselves by positing a unique and go-to shape/contour for ourselves.

Most importantly, it allows us to breathe a sigh of relief that we are not amorphous, nothing is, and that our responsibilities are necessarily delimited and bounded. Not having boundaries is psychological torture. Just as an aside, this is precisely one of the downsides of the internet, that boundlessness which causes great anxiety. Merlin Donald, notwithstanding, exo-graphic repositories of information such as any type of freestanding recording device like art or writing, cannot hold a candle to the following cognitive meta-tool: I intend there to be lines and boundaries, and therefore I anticipate their existence and find what I seek. Contained therein are two of the primary conversion devices—*intention and anticipation*.

POV

Point of View is fascinating. Certainly, to artists who plunk it front and center in their practitioner's toolbox. The abbreviation itself is the name of the most sought-after competition for young filmmakers around these days. When I was making documentaries, I couldn't wait to get the folded invitation. But it succinctly explains what a film is. Obviously, it simultaneously sets up a convoluted duality, that being 'I' over here in this position behind the lens versus the imputed 'I' over there in another position acting out as the audience, be it imagined or documented. And maybe another 'I' floating somewhere within the actual framework of the created content. Certainly, this happens when the editor cuts to the actor's POV but it is more omni present than that. It's a sense of a ringside seat in the middle of all the action taking place in this pseudo world.

I suppose you could go even further and add at least another perspective in there, the mysterious regulator of all these 'selves' that seems to bind them together, determining the status and reliability of each perspective. In other words, if there were nothing to bind these and allow us to nimbly glide between perspectives, then I might believe that I was a rock and that the hands flailing before me and the nose in my field of vision did not belong to me. That the voice coming out of me was not mine. In other words, the understanding of owning a perspective would be entirely discordant, inverted and topsy-turvy. And watching a movie which is really more like participating in a movie becomes very challenging.

The thalamus is often considered the 'regulator' in chief and what James D. Watson of DNA fame considered the hub of consciousness. It allows us to dance between points of view yet keep the continuity of self neatly reined in. Philosophers can be further consulted for the fine-tuning. This is not my wheelhouse.

You needn't be filmmaker or philosopher to get the hang of this POV thing. I recall how my son had this ability in first grade to imagine what something looked like from a different position and draw it. At five, he could draw a bed from the perspective of flying over and around it. His teacher called me in one day and showed me his drawings. She asked me what I thought they were. I was stumped.

They were so odd. Then she explained what he had explained to her. And we were both startled.

I was always terrible at that. Still am. To this very day, I could no sooner do what he did at five with all my drawing experience. In fact, I truly regret not having taken cartooning which is the best hands-on practice for this kind of extreme point-of-viewing. But no one could do it if they didn't have a sense of puppeting their own persona. Neither could you be the cartoonist nor the young child glued to the cartoon screen who fully identifies with it. Remarkable. Totally remarkable.

When neuroscientists address their research about age thresholds for a Theory of Mind, they commonly associate age four to five as the pivot point. But it is startling how they leave out this cultural phenomenon—that at an early age, kids 'get' the extreme viewpoints of cartoon characters. They laugh, they empathize, they are mesmerized. And more important, they are comfortable and at ease. Comfortable - being the key word here.

What makes point of view convoluted is that you cannot have a sense of personal perspective without the implied otherness of everything else. But that also means that we are part of that 'everything else' category too, hence the convolution. Thus, we all predicate the world based on our own status as an object. This is at the heart of separation constructs and the notion of boundaries. No wonder someone with anything resembling Barbara Arrowsmith Young's affliction lived in a world of doubt. I'm guessing that what she was really saying is that she could not 'see' well either.

She had no strategy for clarity or boundaries.

It's harder to execute than to envision

'Ridiculous,' most would say. Everyone can make a mark and mold a face. Hundred-year-olds can and so can toddlers. But that doesn't mean the heading above isn't true. It's just that humans are just good at managing the confusion.

But it really is much harder. In fact, almost impossible because the initial 'flash' of inspiration is a series of quick, nanosecond chains that convey multiple shady images, though we interpret it as singular. And most of us don't care how close we get to the illusion. These imagined visions seem so whole.

However, they are so fleeting and so low resolution that were you to try to refer to it for detailed guidance as you do when drawing from life, Poof! It is gone. In other words, we are so intent on the belief of impactful imagined visualizations, meaning a persistence and solidity to them, when we can no sooner zoom in on the details than we could the pock marks of the moon by looking up at the sky. And not just imagined imagery. Why is it that even when drawing from life, one never returns to precisely the same spot of attention? We certainly do try, but it is without doubt the hardest thing to do in my entire intellectual and sensory life. Excruciatingly so. If you are hard at work drawing the shadow between two fingers in real time, re-finding that shadow on the real object after you have diverted attention to make a mark on paper is pure torture.

When conferring with other extremely articulate artists whose work I admire, they all agree. 'Ay, there's the rub.'

Consider then that the history of art is a long record of invented flourishes that become standardized habits. What we have is a steady stream of styles that sweep up these annoying little details, and broadly suggests, say, what the shadow should be between two fingers because we simply haven't got the intellectual and emotional stamina to do all that heavy lifting. We agitate to pin down other things and cannot steady our visual attention on all the little stuff.

This is why so many resort to tricks like photographic and grid copying because it cuts down on all the ambient noise and confines attention to a framed and flat pattern rather than the presumption of a 'volume' and all that distracting space around it. Photographs calm us for detail work because we are not fighting 'thinking in three dimensions.' All our visual attention is forward and not peripheral. Autists, interestingly enough, do far better with computer tablets for likely the same reason.

> In tablets the keyboard is actually part of the screen, so eye movement from the keyboard to the letter being typed is minimal. Cause and effect have a much clearer correlation. (Grandin 2013:78)

A flat object itself, a photo never moves. And as a result, we do not grapple with projecting ourselves into it. For some reason, *knowing that the 'something' is occupying spatial dimensions challenges our cognition far more than flatness.* More neuro-psych work needs to be done about this dichotomy. There could well be an emotional involvement that retards the complex mimetic process. Our recognition of 'likeness' seems to automatically discard the notion of flatness. And vice versa.

Flat formats are significant for calming the threat of a Theory of Mind. And where was it said that ToM is such a simple and easy concept for us? Because it is not. Why is that?

The real-time effort made when drawing, even when rigorously focused, is whimsical, fleeting, temperamental, fractious, and novelty driven, a cognitive habit of constantly scanned and 'scanning for' information. Our real-time attention cannot sit still. Though you might think that artists look calm, inside they are buzzing with adrenaline because they are overwhelmed.

The rapidity of neural spiking mitigates a sustained idea. When we obsess, we try to sustain a thought against the natural churning of our minds. Like the flashing and pulsing of our computer screens, our brains pulse the imagery so that even if you re-loop or try to sustain an idea, the vast networking of synapses alters it all the time. No one can postulate what the number is per second of action potentials that converts to real-time synaptic neuro transmission.

Let's say we have something like 87 billion neurons. That's not to say all of them are equally engaged at a given moment. Functional MRIs demonstrate this all the time. It's also not to say that each fires as fast as some at 200 times per second, nor how many action potentials convert to leaping the synaptic chasm. Nor for that matter how many dendrites there are per neuron. But let's be ridiculously over-conservative and say that if the brain pulsed out uniformly at 10Hz, or ten times per second (which is incredibly slow), and you multiply that by 87 billion neurons, with a single unique action potential and single unique synapse, you get a number around a trillion spikes per second. That's a tremendous amount of noise and fluctuation.

Except that most scientists believe the more likely number of synapses to be around 100 trillion, and each firing at different rates so that if the flavor of most neurons were at the higher end, say around 200 times per second, you'd have a staggering number of churn - well into the quadrillions.

We don't, though, so relax. That's not the only reason it's hard to suspend a unique visualization long enough to reference it. There are other built-in mitigating factors. Two that readily come to mind. The first is the natural instinct to layer over everything seen with our own sense of corporeal structure. It is unavoidable since every visual field is stealthily framed out by parts of our own body. Just typing these words means I peripherally observe my hands. I have aspects of my glasses in it, my nose and even the scarf around my neck. This semantic knowledge alters the processing of vision. It engages with this solipsism. It predicates the interpretation of all sensations.

We cannot stop doing this just as the vampire cannot resist counting grains. There is an emotional obstruction to get past when we visualize with the intent to replicate. There is still another, more mechanical one that is equally impossible to override.

Novelty

Novelty is a conversion device that drives two of the other ones—anticipation and recursion. We have some kind of a deep-borne repulsion on many behavioral levels for re-experiencing the same thing. Logic asks whether it could be driven in part by our optical physiology.

For example, it is impossible to maintain vision if you try to hold your fixation. I once met a retired engineering professor at Harvard named Richard L. in a lecture. Some philosopher from NYU was there talking about optical fixations. Afterwards, Richard told me he could genuinely fixate without blanking. I was baffled. 'You mean your eyes don't wobble or budge, not even a nano-smidgeon?' Because mine certainly do. Hard as I might, they drift and I'm pretty expert at staring. But I do drift. Is that mechanically caused or cognitively driven by insatiable curiosity on some level. And who isn't curious?

It was further baffling because when fixating, we normally blank out. This means we can no longer see what we were fixating on. By that I also mean that we can no longer concentrate on it with intense attention. The lack of attention that contributes to the blanking is cognitive and might emanate in part from the mental effort to restrain our saccadic curiosity because we are so invested in non-stop harvesting of new visual and mental data.

The systemic importance of continually changing focal points even without moving our body position cannot be glossed over. But for visualizations, it should be used as our cognitive mantra;

visualizing our world is a manic harvesting of just 'enough' information to get the gist of the scene to move on. This 'gist' is often (and superficially) associated with so-called 'zombie behaviors' like driving a car. In many ways, 'the gist' (the 'enough' principle) is the opposite of in-attentional blindness, which we have all experienced, and has nothing to do with the fixational blanking out discussed already.

In-attentional blindness is simpler. There's not a soul alive who doesn't experience this. But just for the record, I remember my 85-year-old aunt calling me up rather upset that she had the first signs of Alzheimer's because she had been searching for her cell phone, anticipating some very important call, and didn't realize it was in her hand. I think it is better to call this attentional blindness because the driver of all these missed observations is that you are overly attentive when anticipating something. This means that you are controlling from the top down rather from the bottom up.

An easy way to understand this is the way we distinguish and guide our own bodies. A top-down version of it is a determination to execute an action. This is called reafferent—sending the cues for self-guidance from within. But that decision to run up the stairs also has a lot do with the size and shape, the height and texture, of the stairs. I might have to alter my top-down plans accordingly. This is contextual or external signaling that I must fully integrate into my propio-ception, and it is called exafferent.

The information or cues are context driven. Neither can we exclusively do one nor the other. Though the lead cues can be tentative and contextual as in stepping along an unknown path, or they can be self-determined as in picking up your child.

Bottom-up observations are exafferent; the salience of the cues resides in the external image or are 'image-immanent,' leading you around the scene rather than by your expectations or your overriding searches. Like waiting for that urgent call so badly that you can't feel the cell phone in your hand. These context-driven cues are also called 'exogenous,' and transiently attract attention regardless of your task. 'Endogenous' cues are in her head about the call she anticipates.

I have a question for you: Does the 'gist' of a scene derive from exogenous or endogenous inspection? Consider that in a mere 30ms, a full apprehension of the entire visual field can be registered, as is done when driving a car.

If the visual notifications are intended to be discarded quickly, is this endogenous, meaning a built-in directive like an arrow pointing to something else. Or is it not? Is it purposeful and essentially a top-down snap shot, a tool that is a pool of information requisite for an overriding task with all minor details necessarily glossed over or you'll crash. One would have to say, 'Yes.'

Wait. Not so fast. If you are navigating by means of less detail and a seemingly top-down decision to work off the 'gist' of things, are you not also more sensitive to less rather than more visual information. Doesn't this also mean that you are also much, much more alert to finer details from which bigger decisions cascade? Yes, you are.

The gist of something is what we use in snapshot to snapshot all day long. It is a mercurial perception of an individual's world that is always guided by purpose to some degree or other. So can we then say that endogenous cues are the ends and exogenous cues are the means? Being ever-mindful of novelty fits neatly into an overarching scheme of anticipation.

In a broader way but likely for the same reasons, one shouldn't think that your brain keeps rolling over the same old visualization equations.

Please don't think that. My idea of a nice, reliable face is never settled law. My idea of what's good-looking isn't either, nor what I consider 'freakish.' Sadly, no fusiform face area experiments track this iconography for one person over time. But they should. What they have tracked is the way people from different generations are forced to respond to a set of standard faces, not necessarily our own idea of a standard face, and that is enormously varied.

The fact is that survival is based on a balancing act between adaptability and norms. Every working cognitive assumption is fragile and transient to some degree. It has to be since our life histories that move us further along also rub against a world in flux. The norms we lay over this flux are essential for tuning out fear and unnecessary distractions to feel safe. But the intersection of my physical and distinctively molting timeline with that of the environment's, asks me to keep looking for new, shorthand recognition routines to expedite my day, my decisions, my longevity.

Anthropology bears this out in counterpoint. Tribal art helps make the point best with its insistent and dogmatic artistic standards trying to fight back and contain straying variations. But even then, it never holds on that long. This is why standardized cultural motifs over time necessarily degrade (read Owen Jones on this). They become hackneyed, morph, and deteriorate because their 'moment' and immediate utility have long passed. They are empty functions.

Cultural motifs, be they dance, dress, language, or in this case, design, perform like a visual fixation that is sustained. What they do is ask you to limit your curiosity, and accept as a given, a standard to which you continually return or fixate. Your normal habits may ask you to consider the same rug design over and over but you notice less and were you in the rug manufacturing wing of your tribe, the execution would become sloppy, the design loose and hackneyed. These design or cultural habits present 'the big picture,' a gloss-over of the finer and smaller nuances of observations and interactions. Thus, they teach less and less.

Now compare this emphatic conceptual view of envisioning the world with the tiny ocular movements we make to refocus our vision.

Take the extreme example of trying to stabilize a retinal image (i.e., focus on something while not restricting saccades, the little jumps or swivels our eyes make to scan and then lock onto a target). Sounds counterintuitive because it is. To do so calls for a lot of bells and whistles. This means that during experiments using contact lens mirrors and prisms, no matter where the eye moves, the image is the same. It's like being followed by a shadowy figure in a dark alley and wherever you turn, he's somehow always there.

In this case, the image follows your gyrations without relief. It is obsessive. Just imagine how annoying, frustrating, even excruciating. Consequently, the photoreceptors at play exhaust themselves and fail to replenish, causing the image to disappear.

Where is the signaling from the thalamus that these are already seen images and no longer pertinent? We don't know yet. And even if the stabilization is fixed to only one eye, inter-ocular transfer to the other eye is diminished.

All of this is by way of telling us that our visual system is novelty-driven. If our optical motoring around a visual field is continuous, how could this training, let alone habit, *not* make semantic the same behavior for trying to conceive imagery? Emphasis on trying.

Imagining is de rigueur fluid and fast-moving. Attending to an ideation is as impossible as being asked to 'hold that thought.' The best we can come up with is a cycling between aspects, sub-clauses of that 'thought' that might be better explained as rhythmically beating it out like a vibration.

As Lewis Nashner explained regarding our motor sensory system, it is a kind of a, '...standardized pattern of stressed and unstressed actions,' meaning the fluctuation back and forth of sub-alternate routines. (Nashner 1985:101–105). Or oscillations, which we now know to be the case for cortical dynamics, though we don't know how pervasive the synaptic rhythm, where the tuner is, or how some cells vary their beats.

This begins to get at what we do when we visualize. Local components or details that you can zoom in on in real-time absolutely do not exist in ideations, though you may want to believe it so. They are purely global and evanescent, though oddly seem to be volumetric. This should give us a clue as to where three-dimensional 'viewing' originates. It is not a stereoscopic phenomenon; it is a cognitive fiat. This means 'I think I can' conjure up my mother's face from several angles when she smiled. I just can't get 'close enough' to see how light falls on her mouth, or exactly the shape of her eyes. I can't break it apart. They are simplified and thus iconic.

Artists know this better than most, which is what the so-called creative struggle is all about. Specification always collapses the function of the whole. This suggests that whatever a given visual might be, it is not solely 'flashing' in the ventral visual system that favors shape and color, nor is it constructed exclusively in the dorsal stream where motion imagery and prosody are deciphered. The neurons supplying this rough imagery are dispersed throughout the brain, beginning somewhere in the neocortex, no doubt. The typical monitoring or 'correlation' done by the Lateral Geniculate Nucleus (LGN) of the Thalamus, the normal arbiter of input channeling from the retina to the primary visual system, has to yield over much of its managerial powers.

Syntactical language production is believed by many to derive from a gestural lexicon. As further support of this, even the shadows of hand signals are registered as symbolic motions, provided they are not whimsical but rather to be advertising purpose.

Purpose or 'meaning' is implied as causative or goal-oriented. What do I make of my mother's face smiling at me? Is it a shape-dominating event, because that seems to be all I can manage to concentrate on even though I can easily make it move?

Anecdotally speaking (a scientific no-no), I posit that it is diffuse. Why? Because to 'hold' or freeze the image, it has the feeling of pulsing in and out of mind, a flashing. Retinoptically speaking, flashing shows a bit of favoritism for the MT+ or Dorsal stream and is construed as a form of motion. But I am not parsing incoming light waves with direction-sensitive cells as I would normally do in my primary visual cortex, and my V5 motion center, am I? The fact is, I just don't have an answer.

One thing I do know is that it is both so particular yet evanescent as to insist that the only way to begin to sustain and capture it requires mnemonics (i.e., glossed-over characterizations or equivalencies). These are kinds of 'symbols.' To recall her face, I must start with a typical and general caricature. But symbols are a wide-spectrum phenomenon. They needn't be static, or even reusable. They just need to be 'enough.' A kind of vessel into which can be poured any variety of details as long as the general contour and a few inner specifics are obtained. Like an upturned sharp jaw and wide-set almond eyes. They are not the same as explicit narrative symbolism by which many in the field determine we achieve sufficient specificity to correlate robust equations within standardized object categories.

Christian iconography being a case, with a whole lexicon of very specific equivalencies. I inherited a small, old dictionary on the subject, but there are more recent ones that run into a thousand pages. The easy ones are the palm leaf for martyrdom, the lamb for the Christ child. It doesn't matter how you delineate them, the believers, most of whom could not read words, could certainly read the narrative by means of symbolic graphics.

If you try to regain the image with all the other distractions going on in your life and body, then you reenter the thought thread at a different point in time and neural synapsing. This might have something to do with what many like Michael Corballis believe to be our most sophisticated mental attribute, that being 'time traveling.' This is the ability to enter and reenter events from different temporal and spatial windows, to mix and remix them based on one's personal or episodic history. It's like the adage that you can't put your foot in the same water twice. So, you issue equivalency prompts, like icons, words, caricatures, which tend to be left brain and responsive in the extrastriate cortex of the inferior temporal gyrus.

When I tried to draw my mother's face before she passed away, I was pulling out an image of her smiling that had momentous influence on me at the time. I was traveling back and forth in time, but in a very linear way. If you drew the course of my route, it would be just that, a route. A line.

Because of this and by means of this emotional context, I was formulating an icon that I would continually loop to remember her by. The entry point for that icon was largely flat. It was a frontal face and specifically positioned to be upward-pointing toward me.

However, when consulting this for the purpose of rendering 'it,' I simply was unable to make it specific enough, though it seemed so at the time, in fact every time I called up the prompt. The reason is that the activity of drawing is a linear Chaîne Opératoire of several connected activities, but on multimodal levels. Step follows step. A far better way of thinking about this is as an oscillating directional flow that gathers steam by pulsing information back and forth as I shift from neural resources to motor actions and back again.

Conversion Devices

PART THREE

Let me explain.

Making the mark is a separate action that diverts your attention from the ideation. All 'marking' and 'making' is a shift away from the mental image to a remembered image. Thus, it requires time traveling by allowing us to embed remembered ideas and cranking forward with new ones. It has to be because the contexts and the motor system you use are entirely different. The least of the confusion being that of holding a tool and then placing it on the faux map you are creating, which is none other than the plastic image you are fabricating. But you cannot fabricate a map unless you are jockeying others.

What makes it extremely difficult to do, and the reason that so few are truly good at drawing from life, for example, is the neuronal issue at play in the hippocampus, a component of the limbic system in the medial temporal lobe. And more specifically, a strange-shaped component of it; a wishbone-like cell cluster whimsically named because of its two ram-like horns that resemble the ancient Egyptian god Amun's zoomorphic identity as a ram. This section called Cornu Amon (Cornu Amonnis), or the horns of Amon, represents the CA part of its full terminology, CA1.

It sports the same breed of pyramidal cells that defines much of the neocortex, and as a fellow participant in the limbic system, the amygdala. And just as an aside, these CA1 cells are excitatory and of probably two distinct categories found to be such through disparate firing patterns or oscillations of their synapses. We know this because the hippocampus is known in humans for a distinctly robust EEG signal. A theta wave cycle that distinguishes the hippocampus, particularly. Theta cycles being low frequency pulses of 6Hz to 10Hz per second.

In rats, a single pyramidal in their CA1 version has a remarkable ratio, where its 12,000 dendrites receive approximately 30,000 excitatory inputs versus the rather paltry 1700 of inhibitory ones.

Drilling down further, this means that research has revealed in the hippocampal pyramidal cells that some fire outputs in bursts of large irregular activity (LIA) and some fire outputs in regular slow activity called theta cycles (Graves et al 2012; Buzsaki 2002). Austin Graves et al changed the nomenclature to call these, respectively, early bursting spiking and late-bursting.

I mention this only to give some color as to what's at play in a complex mapping of self in a variety of terms that include temporal sequencing. The temporal sequencing is, as I have often mentioned, a chained link of minute memorizing on which short-term memory is based. If I am immediately recalling putting my sock on and then my shoe, the sequencing is the basis for the memory itself. In the same way, the spatial mapping of self, where my foot is at different degrees of actions, is also as basic to short-term memory.

The two components of temporal sequencing and spatial mapping are largely the same. They seem to interchange duties. For example, when we review a video clip, which has now obviously become a memory, time-sequencing cells fire. This is borne out in work done on the hippocampus, which has long been known to be the vessel for short-term memory, out of which flows archiving of declarative memories to the prefrontal cortex when experiences are deemed important enough.

Further sorting results. Mapping is self-locating in terms of other things and always involves short-term memory and sequential threading. By that I mean the firing of specific cells registering the sequence of a memory or procedure of locating one's own progress—what happens before, after, and in between. For example, recent experiments have shown that:

> ...spatial coding observed as rats actively run through a maze recapitulated in temporally coded firing sequences when the rat is not moving. Disruption of these replay events impairs subsequent memory of the path. (Eichenbaum 2014)

If the time sequence is broken, the memory collapses. Creating something involves all of this. When one draws, there is a constant impairment of the memory path because we have to constantly re-find our physical self, vis-à-vis a frontal format like a canvas or plastic form with hand motions and the manipulation of tools. We must compare the tool location on the tangible field with our sensory motor system's *own* mapping out of where we sense our own physical extensions such as where hand and general bodily placements are.

Thus, the replay of that short-term memory for executing a small path as a line on a face involves hippocampal time and place cells in the CA1 area that are constantly in need of recharging because the remapping underway necessarily disrupts the immediately former temporal sequencing and all becomes a jumble.

This means our short memory of, let's say, the contour of a face is excruciatingly hard to re-find because of all the time with place cell interruptions.

To give further evidence as to just how involved (make that overworked) the hippocampus is when something like drawing from life is involved, consider findings reported by Howard Eichenbaum. Activation of the hippocampus in humans occurs during:

> Encoding of overlapping face sequences, remembering the order of objects visited in a virtual environment, reconstruction of the order of scenes in a movie clip, retrieval of overlapping and non-overlapping face sequences, viewing of items out of order in a familiar sequence.... (Eichenbaum 2014:10)

And I just cannot resist this one, '...disambiguation of overlapping routes through a virtual maze.' Any kind of mark-making, in this case of drawing, is precisely a mental exertion of separating overlapping routes of where to visually re-find the points of interest like the nose we were trying to draw *and* re-finding the routes on paper or any material, and even more taxing, of reestablishing a procedure for continuing to craft new ones.

Is the theta-throbbing of our hippocampus derived from within the hippocampus or externally from other regions? Are the apparently uniquely designated pyramidal cells for place versus time in combat? Or is this excitatory neural complex yielding predominance to one cell type over the other given the task at hand? Clearly, there have been found to be two variants, bursting cells, with extensive tuft (apex) dendrites, and regular spiking cells, with more basal dendrites.

And it goes on and on. We think it is simple, but if it were, we could juggle the fabricating of the image better and never lose 'sight' of the originating mental impulse. Or the visual prompts. There would be no rhythmic alternating of stressed and unstressed actions. The fact is that either drawing from life or just mind, I have become so utterly distracted by the physical activity of mediating so many overlapping maps in real-time that I cannot return to it as originally intended. The short-term memory is thus compromised. This shifting of an accretive physical process back and forth with a mnemonic one further derogates the initial inspiration.

Ideations or flashes of imagery that we use as impulses for inspiring creativity are fleeting caricatures, summations or designs that result from active and very personal recognition habits about aspects of our world. They are emphatic and generalized. But just because they are generalized, one shouldn't dismiss them as 'lame.' Because none of them are weak nor nebulous, the reason being that we are always 'thinking' about salience, stewing 'emphasis' on a back mental burner regarding the objects in our world.

These are really categorization techniques that expedite recognition. Toulouse Lautrec tried to explain to his cousin Gabriel that art is not about some silly novel technique, but rather '...novelty is hardly ever important. What matters is always just the one thing: To penetrate to the very heart of a thing and create it better' (Arnold 2004:90). By better, you might also swap 'easier' or 'faster.' 'Penetrating to the very heart of the thing' does not mean tricking it out with details. On the contrary, it means figuring out the essential combinations of strokes, be they 2D or 3D, that cut immediately to the right spot in our recognition catalog.

What does it really mean to envision?

When we imagine something, is there an immediate, automatic, built-in somatosensory response that 'feels' like some kind of personal motion? Let me answer this one for you, 'Not much, if at all.' 'Imagining' is a wide-berth, somatosensory form of in-attentional blindness. We lose sensations of our body when we concentrate on the inner picture. When the task changes, though, so does the somatosensory blindness. Okay, then. But when we concentrate on seeing something real-time, do we respond to it in our joints and muscles? A bit, maybe in ways that are so hard to corroborate with neural specificity that most would likely say, 'Not at all.' And maybe one reason for this is that life goes by so fast that we can't notice all that much.

But it does exist and part of that kinesthetic response is a subtle spatial one in which we are evaluating location and distances from ourselves. We are inventing them too. Most scientists devise experiments to smoke this out as a separate visual function but fail to understand the 'why' part of our need to evaluate spatial contexts in the first place. Those visuospatial assessments are constantly discussed in terms of our working memory apparatus, something for which Alan Baddeley and Graham Hitch devised a new model in 1974.

Firstly, they suggested a sound and language loop, a visual loop and an episodic or personalized and autobiographic, long-term memory loop, all of which were orchestrated by a 'central executive' in the pre-frontal cortex.

Let's briefly talk about working memory, how robust it is, how long it lasts, and what it assesses. Into the episodic loop - they piled in multimodal influences and semantic memory, the tacit stuff by which we use to operate daily. Their first step was important for discussing art. They ascertained that the visual loop by which we devise spatial notifications in order to self-navigate, posit distances between things, and remember locations should be called a sketch pad, a short-term visual memory component.

Then in 1990, Alan Baddeley and Robert H. Logie (and others) determined through experiments that certain responses crowded out functionality. Meaning they called on the same neurons to do certain tasks, and that certain other challenges were fluid and allowed for swifter recall because they were not neurally contravening.

They came up with a further breakdown in the visual sketchpad idea, one rather consistent with the dorso-ventral motif of vision comprised of a 'where' motion stream (i.e., dorsal) and a 'what' object cache (i.e., ventral). They maintained that there is an 'inner scribe,' which includes movements like scanning, motion toward a target, and motions of objects among themselves. The other one they logically called the 'visual cache' (i.e., colors, shapes). Logie elaborated on the distinctions between the cache and the inner scribe, all of which information was a part of working memory if it could be sustained or rehearsed long enough, and then onto long-term memory if it could be linked, also known as 'chunked,' with some trigger in our personal narrative archives.

Along comes Stephen Luck and Edward Vogel in 1997 who discovered that we briefly hold visual information to a limit of four components capacity which was also orchestrated in some way by the prefrontal cortex executive. EEGs were strapped on to confirm the activity in these general areas. Their findings? That this capacity was object-based, but not restricted to features within each object.

Question: How do you define the difference between a feature and an object? More importantly, when drawing or when creating anything, which is an analog procedure of sequenced actions, how is the shadow under the neck not an object? Answer: It is. A feature is very much an object. And this is why there is such a bottleneck in transfer or conversion behaviors from idea to plastic form.

The bottleneck is within that so-called four-part, short-term memory capacity; the details themselves interrupt and use the same neural architecture. They are all dealing with conjunctions of sorts; where colors border colors, where shapes meet shapes, and all perceived in some manner as the junction of lines. There is a high cognitive activity at play such that there is an observed reduction of set size capacity due to the overload. In other words, I can remember a round circle easily, and a mosquito. But in one studied glance, if I have to draw the junction of an armpit to the upper torso I see on the model, it wipes out my capacity to also remember what her elbow looks like. The spatial assessments for shape junctions crowd each other out. Not so if I wanted to remember a letter AND a spatial assessment. The visual complexity sensitivities reside in part in the superior parietal and lateral occipital areas.

These difficulties are legion. This is why I have to put forward the following quote in italics from Georg Goldenberg.

> *'It seems to me that imagery is still in search of a theory.'*

Ah, yes. Time and technology will tell. Being able to zoom in on individual cells will certainly help.

The Fab Four:

Novelty, Intention, Recursion and... Mirroring

It is when we seek to imitate to any degree whatsoever that we innervate vestibular, propio-sensory, and kinesthetic nerves. We activate certain neural hubs over which we seem to have little control. This suggests that mimesis as a source of creating art is unavoidable, originating as it does in micro-reflexes that are genetic traits.

This endless referring back that we do depends on a deeply reflexive system called 'mirroring'. Mirroring, as observed from the innervation of neurons in the Rhesus Macaque's ventral premotor cortex, occurs when they observe a human or other monkey picking something up. It was then suggested by a number of scientists at the University of Parma that the human homologue for this resided in our linguistic generator called Broca's area (see Chapter 3).

When seen in its basic form through the Macaque brain, we find that;

> It seems likely that Broca's area, and its primate homologue, played a critical role in the shift from manual to vocal gesture. Some of the neurons in area F5 in the

> monkey respond both when the animal makes reaching movements to pick up an object and when the monkey observes another individual making the same movement, and these neurons are now understood to be part of a more general 'mirror system' in the monkey brain. (Corballis 2010:115–123)

Before proceeding, let's establish a bit of a baseline for reliable comparisons. For starters, just how reliable *is* the macaque monkey model for us?

Richard Passingham, Emeritus Fellow at Oxford University, has warned that when using voxels to compare, these little cubic bytes are clusters of millions of neurons. Which means that fundamentals are too coarse for fully understanding the monkey mechanisms, let alone ours.

Further, he warns, '...Aspects of the micro-structure of the human brain (cannot) be accounted for by differences in size' (Passingham 2009). And that Brodmann's 32, the dorsal para-cingulate area in humans, which activates when we reflect on mental states, has no homologue in the macaque. Second and most importantly, no spindle cells or Von Economo's are found in their anterior insulae as there are in humans. Bottom line? We have little other choice given the ethical restrictions for probing humans. So 'pioneer' work has to proceed accordingly. I will add one more thing, that the differences are far more illustrative than the similarities.

'Mirroring' is a behavior that derives from neural redundancies that construct our basic syntactical phrasing. By 'Syntax' I mean an established procedure that affects the transmission of understanding. And 'syntactical phrasing' because there has to be a deeply ingrained, cognitive routine that can 'call up' the imitation or the 'mirroring' in the first place.

For example, if I have never felt what being 'large' is, how can I call up the sensation and apply it to the largeness of say an elephant for being substantially different or greater than my own little self? I am enormous in comparison to a grain of sand, which is also as different from me as anything could be. The syntax has to reference myself first before it can conceive of exterior likenesses and before finally returning back to myself for final comparisons.

There likely are many more subtle steps in between, but we tend to like listing things with three reasons. For now, three-part syntax that underscores our mirroring impulse will have to do. Nevertheless, it is a complete thought sentence - establishing the main point, switching it up for color, and dangling something a bit different such as that 'other likeness.' Which in turn alters the original precept - oneself - with a new filter.

In much simpler terms, it goes like this: I want to mimic my friend walking. Once I establish some basis for the likeness to begin with, I mimic her, and as a result, immediately alter my concept for 'self' based on this new behavior.

If you reverse or tamper with the embedded coding sequences, you'll never capture the sensation of sizing or imitating someone else walking. Luckily, most normal people can't tamper with it. The syntax (i.e., the route by which we make these determinations) is so rigid and deeply anchored in a particular part of the brain (perhaps others too), that there are no other ways to express the wonder of nature's enormity and mystery other than bouncing it off oneself.

For one thing, and only a tiny one thing, recent data suggest that this phrasing derives from the aforementioned basic premise of projecting the 'I am' sensation as 'that' object when it is another human being or animal whose close physical attributes (i.e., eyes, nose, mouth, four limbs, etc.) makes this an easy extrapolation.

Nevertheless, as Paul Simon sang, 'I am a rock, I am island.' What we have constructed off this remarkably simple phrase is the stuff of our creative grandeur.

And it is this implicit phrasing that is perhaps the *modus operandi* for the structuring of components and which comprise what Marc D. Hauser calls 'discrete infinity' (Hauser 2002: 1569–1571). This is the mutuality of understanding in communication, whereby discreet units can be infinitely arranged yet understood because of overriding syntactical rules. These rules would have no substance without the core property, at least to me, of this recursive little dynamic phrase, implied or stated.

Unfortunately, for so many scholars and writers (the citations are far too numerous to note), they get distracted by the penumbra of recursive behavior—the activity of generating hierarchies of embedded ideas that ultimately represent an image but base it purely on verbal communication (see all of Pinker and Hoffecker 2007).

But recursive thinking and activity was highly prominent among the two-million-year-old hominin knappers, who had to think about 'where to place *me* (i.e., my hand and arm motions) in terms of locating a point on *that* (i.e., the unformed core).' Making these things into bifacial entities (about 1.5 million years ago) furthered this mirroring of human symmetry, of balance, and of projecting some incredibly specific ideation of an object as four dimensions—length, width, depth, and time. To do this, they had to have had a shadow notion of themselves as a like volumetric object to predicate this. Once this is done, it is really not such a huge and remarkable cognitive leap to compare oneself to a gazelle and thereby mediate this impersonation with lines and colors. Below is an artist's description of drawing her cat:

> I draw spontaneously, absorbing the subject matter, impersonating it inwardly, feeling its inflection and structure—as with music—and then enacting it using marks. As soon as I begin I have two more tools; accident and improvisation. The intense combination of observation and improvisation creates something like a spell. It's a marvelous condition. (Jay Brady, Artist Statement for *Gallery Small New York* 2011)

That condition of impersonating it inwardly is the 'dope' of creative endeavor. For the most *successful* artists, a standard I shall discuss later, this activity is exhausting. We are actors, though the stage is plastic, but actors nonetheless. It rests on this blending of ego boundaries with anything else. The result is an attentional ferocity that travels between mapping out the elision of one's space volume with another's.

And while some like Brady call it 'marvelous,' others like myself call it hyper-frenetic, messy, and exhausting. And so exasperating because of this seesawing between perspectives—one definite, namely oneself, and the 'other' imputed. It is a time-consuming and extremely clumsy process. But were you to interrupt me or her as we draw, you would find us to be dangling somewhere en route to or from the object of interest.

It is a semantic habit brought front and center and made highly conscious by the creative acting that art is. Refocusing your attention in either perspective, that being whether you sense you are more over there or more over here (i.e., in yourself), causes you to lose your place on the new 'map' you are drawing. Re-finding it again and again is the hard part. But all of us do it in practically every movement we make, and mostly unconsciously. The complexity of this cognito-sensory amalgam is so intricate, it requires a lot of research and experiments to peel all the layering.

Juggling Foci

Creating art *per se* is one of those endeavors that rationalizes our neurological reflex to anticipate responses in other things. It is a pure play on this principle, and while many like to talk about the 'meaning' of an image, the narrative components, the philosophical riffs, and expressions, at its core is this dramatizing of our innate need to adopt perspectives. Juggling foci is not easy, and it takes a tremendous amount of orderly thought, of delayed solutions, of compartmentalizing embedded structures, of decisions about emphasis. This is not so much about where and how to place a line, but rather the opposite. An efferent sense of where not to place it, a self-correcting monitor for all the myriad of meta-solutions combined that is guided from within the head.

The technique of knowing where not to apply the marks is the domain of 'working memory,' which lasts a few short seconds. It also depends on the sophistication of my executive function skills to orchestrate so many operations toward a greater goal. That greater goal I seem to have to hold in abeyance. I have to park the ideation somewhere on the back burner and invent millions of meta-tools in the form of marks and colors and shapes that 'solve' the underlying dilemma. Not to lose access to it.

> In human evolution, the complexity of tool behavior increases regarding the number of active foci managed at a time in an action, the number and diversity of operational steps in a problem solving complex, and the spatial temporal frame in which solutions are sought. (Miriam Haidle 2010)

In other words, juggling foci, as I have just described, is itself a tool-making behavior. Forget 'Material Archaeology' and understand that

108

the great and signature meta tools are in our heads. It's what some like Wolfgang Kohler in 1926 called 'indirect thinking.' If your motivation is to slay a deer, then you need an arrow, the making of which occupies considerable time and effort and thinking before you can return to the original goal. I wouldn't call it 'indirect,' but rather 'abeyant cognition,' where short-term thinking departs from '...the immediate problem and shift(s) to abstract conceptualizations of potential solutions which results in sequences of physical actions...' (Haidle 2010:153).

All of this sounds so dry that if I have to 'think' about shuttling between foci rather than just drilling down to get to the meat of it, I wouldn't be able to execute a darn image. However, that guiding 'abeyant' idea, or the 'meat of it,' is not so discreet and bold, nor as instructional as you might think. Were the foci distinctly bounded and lying unmoved like two boulders in the sand, we'd probably never have been interested in it in the first place. The reason is that our brains defy static imagining.

Prompting the Mental Image

Let's get something cleared up. 'Prompting' is different than 'priming.' The latter is a 'setup' to expedite recall. It introduces in a variety of ways exactly what you want someone to find. In other words, it's a hint. 'Prompting' recall is not a premeditated manipulation of outcomes. It is an association that triggers recall and depends on how robust it is to some aspect of a specific memory.

'Doodling' is an incredibly direct way to reveal the categorical prompts we archive for imaging. By doodling, I do not mean the little cartoons students draw. I mean the seeming undirected scribbling across a page without lifting the pencil. It involves fuller use of the arm and hand than the little icons kids draw. It tends to be vigorous and enjoyably unrestricted.

Depending on the experience and temperament of the player, these (supposedly) carefree marks and often messy nexuses of lines will directly strike the implicit targets or simplistic iconography we lump into broad working categories. This becomes apparent when asked to 'find' objects within their mess, though our tendency is to find them anyway. Keep in mind the notion that we might have been obliquely drawing them anyway. Yes, these funny squiggles do prompt but isn't it really because they are priming first?

The lines themselves often start as entoptic-type scribbles (e.g., zags, swirls, meanders, hatching, circles, and triangles), which we then coalesce into tight, recognizable forms. They can just as often elicit memories and potentials of more specific and unique object details. For example, kids will usually end up with their own derivative little caricatures from the initial wandering marks during math class or a boring lecture on Medieval feudalism.

Doodling, therefore, would seem to fit more into this dynamic of shifting foci and resurrecting abeyant images because the whole premise is based on more randomness and less 'direct thinking.' This sounds incredibly counterintuitive, but the reality is that it has a purity and directness about the way our brains process visualization. In fact, it is a good experimental foundation for peeling away some of those layers of categorical icons. It allows for getting to the heart of implicit versus explicit images.

The random marks trigger a personal ideated response. There is no originating inspiration other than dragging a marker across a paper. No self-conscious impersonating of some other object or person. No compulsive mimesis.

But could anything, any use of a tool like pencil to paper, even if your eyes are closed, ever be pure and not stealthily manipulated on some remote level?

Consider another kind of doodling. I like to mention this manner of image-fabrication because I derive a lot of my own work from it and used it all the time when teaching high school art classes to break down their fad-inspired idiosyncrasies.

It begins with vigorous, even close-eyed, scribbling all over the paper. Switch papers to your neighbor. Then the squinting of eyes to let the mind resurrect anything abeyant. Why squinting? Because it is looking for some cue to emerge and link with our visual archives and of letting priming become prompting. Scanning across all of this 'mess' necessarily asks for a cognitive 'answer.' And answers are constructive. They format data.

Recall that our brains like to conserve mental energy. We especially abhor visual dysfunction because most of our information is derived visually. We are depending on our eye inputs to be reliable and useful. Visual dysfunction would mean that our visual acumen lacks purpose, that it is unpinned. Which also means that 'it' or we fail to disambiguate and make sense of the world. Which also means that a high level of entropy, or the inevitable decomposing of order into randomness, prevails. And we flail at everything requiring a greater amount of energy to convert chaos into an orderly working system.

But our brains reject this haziness because accepting it would mean a huge energy investment to resurrect some semblance of order constantly just to get anything done or known. Thus, we must presume there to be order a priori rather than the need to invent it. In humans, this subconscious directive is always much closer to conscious awareness that of questing for confirmation of order because we insist it to be so. A choice that is far better and certainly more energy-efficient than constantly straining to seek directionless direction. But the deep inroads of efficiencies in our brains like the visual system's orientation columns uncovered by Hubel and Weisel take care of a lot of Sturm and Drang.

***

Certain lines and shapes are more prominent disambiguation triggers than others. Further, the mind is context-driven and predisposed to certain salient iconography, depending on our mood, time of day, and immediate priming like real-time patterns on clothes, architecture, faces, etc. Couple that with our manic 'follow-the-leader' brain—whatever is or has been in our face most recently seems to be that which we think we are originating on our own. What entices about this exercise is the presumption of random disorder and the challenge to apply one's own shape lexicon.

There are some questions to consider about this exercise:

1. Does the directive to 'find something' immediately make this a top-down exercise?

2. If so, how does that reconcile with associating preexisting lines and shapes on the paper that are not clearly priming the search?

3. Are they mostly perceiving on their own terms or are they recognizing based on a more superficial layer of trending memes?

4. Which part of their brain lights up the most with the understanding that recognition is a pervasive enterprise largely involving associations across the extrastriate in the temporal lobes.

5. Given the confusing look of the scribbling, how can they then recognize something if they were not first taught to understand spatial boundaries and the inherent circumscribing of them with line concepts (*Pat the Bunny*, reaching and

touching, etc.) Also, how is their visual spatial working memory functioning? It must be overdrive.

6. Are they pressed to integrate more than associate? Meaning are they making their selections as close to universal standardizations or paradigms, or are they integrating the lines to form extreme variants on a theme like a strange kind of fantastical face?

7. How are we culling salience from our stored ideas; is it in three dimensions or flat and frontally based on external formats we have seen before?

8. And perhaps most important, what line(s) segments prompted the association?

***

Remove the doodling. Here's a seemingly farfetched question, is it possible there could be prompts on a flat white page? After all anything frontal and fully attended jogs our brain. And the reality is that our eyes see so many variations, lights, and darks that could also technically inspire a form. But it never does. The spots of light and dark are a result of our center surround retinal cells, half of which turn off the light and half of which turn up the light. The reason is that the overall distribution confounds our ability to extricate forms from it. We gloss over the contrasting uniformity and move onto the lines.

However, autists can't stand this. Their visual system is overly sensitive to shine or light refraction such that a great many of them sense sparks streaming forth in these circumstances which includes bright white surfaces. Anything put down on these kinds of formats is highly irritating, causing in some cases a sensation of letters jiggling on paper if not the entire world. Therefore, Temple Grandin suggests they avoid contrasting colors, avoid multicolor tiles and lattices. She suggests they avoid fluorescent light flickering at 50 Hz to 60 Hz, where peripheral vision is more responsive due to the luminance sensitivity of rods over cones. This is consistent with many autists preferring to look askance out of the corner of their eyes because they see better that way. Perhaps they don't really 'see' better, they just feel more comfortable that way because color contrast through the cones is too much information for them.

This is one reason Grandin also suggests they assuage the perceived brightness and contrast with tinted glasses or use grey/pale green paper that allows them to concentrate and 'see' much better. Highly contrasted visuals can be annoying, but they are really a subjective thing. 'Contrast' is the juxtaposition of the measurable luminance or reflected light off the source itself. As already mentioned, it can be understood as the distance between the intensity of the colors or hues purely in terms of the measured light emitted. For example, if you kept the colors on the screen and removed their pigmented hues, or printed them on a black and white printer, what shades of grey would they be? And how different in gray scale would they be from each other? This is contrast.

*

The question becomes, 'Exactly what part of the retinal cells is overwhelmed?' Is there a preponderance of cones firing off too much information? After all, cones are much better than rods at detecting light flickering. Are horizontal connections over- or under-firing? Clearly there is a preference for lower light waves, and especially peripheral seeing.

> I've asked kids, 'Why do you look out from the corner of
> your eyes?' They say, 'Because I can see better that way.'
> As for why they can see better that way, I don't know....

Because the world is moving too fast and a sidelong glance makes all the motion less over-whelming? Maybe. (Grandin 2012: 84)

Time will tell us the answer.

Color

C.J. Munro to James Clerk Maxwell, March 3ʳᵈ, 1871

I wish you...could eradicate the insane trick of reasoning about colors as identified by names. People seem to think that blue is blue.... (Ings 2008)

I too have become extremely aware of this ocular contrasting off bright white surfaces like my computer screen or drawing paper, and sometimes launch my efforts off this dynamic and swirling clutter of suggestions. Yes, for me there are suggestions in the dotted contrasts in a white color field though highly subliminal.

Unfortunately, our hectic and complex lives have asked us to 'believe' that 'color' means there is one flat color and to discard the notion of luminance entirely, which is impossible. It takes a lot of something else to override the gradations of brightness.

Again, we bring up the notion of conservation of mental energy. This might be one reason we have acclimated to expedited visualization among expedited living, generally. These beliefs are cultural fads as much as they are modes of 'seeing,' where neocortical habits mediate the terms of knowledge by which we operate. The STROOP test is the most common example of this, where reading the color of ink used overrides our ability to visually identify and then name it.

The test singles out a strident interference of tasking where two pre-potent habits collide head-on and one must be suppressed or inhibited to suppress an error in execution. That potential error is defined by the instruction of the task at hand. In other words, what you are being told to do or are telling yourself to do. In this case, a habitual or pre-potent response as in reading is being consciously suppressed and moreover replaced by a non-conditioned, multimodal response that is far more complex a cognitive task. Such is visualizing, identifying, and naming for color of a font for which we are never used to doing.

How often do we mentally peck around to name a specific color other than the primaries? Rarely. But the Stroop test asks only for primaries not, nuanced colors, which raises a red flag on the enormous limitation of the testing to date.

How often do we read abstract forms, as are letters, that trigger speech responses? All the time. If you print the word 'red' using blue ink and asked to only name the color, either verbally or by pushing a button, both coalescing in motor responses, you are momentarily confused. Two entrenched habits battle it out with a specific portion of the anterior cingulate gyrus monitoring the conflict to deliver an error-free resolution.

Consequently, a pronounced confusion in performance priorities causes an interference in understanding. As Jose Pardo says:

> The task demands resolution of a conflict between two competing tendencies... and a limited capacity attentional system in the selection of processing appropriate for job execution. (Pardo 2004:256)

Positron emission tomography, or PET, tracks blood flow ratios in neural regions rather than by specific neurons. Nevertheless, it reveals pronounced local activity. In this case, especially in the anterior cingulate cortex, and even more so in the dorsal portion, among less-activated areas like the prefrontal cortex and left premotor cortex. Much of the confusion results from the anticipation of object attributes in a variety of contexts not aligning with the on-spot inspection. This requires the inhibition of an innate or pre-potent response.

As an aside, activation also occurs when the error is executed and doubt persists or FRN (feedback related negativity), as when the error is detected after the fact. OCD is known for activating the ACC, especially in the rostral area and for the obsession about doubt and second-guessing choices stated above. In this case, there is an error-related negativity response to actions that is measurable by blood flow, both for error-related actions and as correct actions, and is highly consistent with their sense of always doubting their behavior or that of the world around.

One would then surmise that in autistic spectrum disorders, where the observation is typically of their inability to self-correct or appropriately respond to events, that the amplitude and activity of their ERN is both flatter and latent, which has been duly noted (Thakkar et al 2008:2464).

I suggest that if the Stroop task were worded differently (i.e., to name the color of the *letters* rather than the word), the conflict in tendencies would be far less. And if the task were to name the color, where the color was not a primary, nor the word a primary color word, we might see far less activation in the ACC, the emphasis being on a local description rather than a symbol. This would be quite revealing and less semantic dueling would be present. Symbols are ways to strategize and conserve mental energy efficiently. By not using these prompts, we are not depending on conserving mental energies because the task is already asking us to go beyond that.

***

Think of how nice it is that primitive tribes have fewer color words. 'Less is more,' as they say, and sure enough, fewer words allows them to understand how we see, perhaps much better, but certainly more honestly, and in tune to the physical sensations involved. Because with less broad a color palette formed by habit, they cannot get tripped up by a deeply ingrained habit that supersedes a clear and present task. They can combine, nuance, and name in detail more accurately based on the present challenge rather than the entanglements of a deeply ingrained reflex. This has to do with texture, reflection, and time of day, consistent with the ebb and flow of light. It allows them to covet the utility and volume of the object with a certain fondness, with emotions of relief, of comfort, etc. *because* enough time is invested in 'knowing' all about it. And when this kind of broad- based thinking is harnessed, it is far easier to name the colors.

Thus, it is less implicit and less confused by extensive and insistent verbal labeling. Labeling that prejudices expectations of color as symbols or pre-judgments, which trump any kind of nuanced sensation. One might ask the obvious question: Have we designed a modern world driven by expectations alone of top-down labeling as opposed to nuance? I think you know the answer.

When compared to say the ancient Greeks, for example, Homer famously called the Blue Mediterranean, 'wine dark.' Well, to be honest, that is what we think he did because in 1843 Henry George Liddel, the Chancellor of Christ Church, Oxford University, translated it that way. As Caroline Alexander points out in her *Lapham Quarterly* article, 'A Wine-like Sea,' the term Homer used was 'oínopa pónton.' Oínopa is a compound of 'wine' and 'eye.' Meaning 'a wine color to-the-eye.' She translates it as 'wine-faced,' and thus 'wine-ish.'

But we artists know better. It's all about 'to the eye.' And 'to the eye' always has to do with 'to the brain' (i.e., contextualized feelings). Emotions, subtle or in your face, always alter our interpretation of color. And emotions are linked to so many other factors like time of day, relationships, and whether you just happened to hop out of bed extremely bummed, happy, or hungry, or stubbed your toe.

Homer just called it 'wine-ish.' But how do you get something we moderns stereotype as a maroon and purple color for a watery mass we also stereotype as a blue, navy blue, and then black at night? No, his sentiment was far darker, steeped in a complex sense of vulnerability, of adventure, of foreboding, and death that any high sea threatens. *Pónton* means the 'open sea.' In this case, it's associated with a specific narrative, and of anxiety triggered by the ebb and flow of a day and ominous portending. Homer also called it 'melas,' from which we get melancholy, a sense of pervasive greyness.

This is why Caroline Alexander suggests the Greeks were more descriptive of light effects than hue. That their 'colors' were really reflection sensations, like darkness, brightness, glints, shadows, sparkles, etc. Her idea is well taken. In 1858, William Gladstone decided to do a color term search of the Odyssey and found that 'black' was mentioned 200 times, white or bright was mentioned 100 times, and very minimally red and then yellow. Though iron and sheep are described as violet. Honey is green. Blue is never mentioned despite being so vast a presence and seems to be rarely mentioned throughout the human record in both developed and developing societies.

Even today, Namibians have no word for it, and ascribe it to the green color field. The reason seems obvious, that their sensitivity for greenness is paramount in their lives and far exceeds our dependence on the behavior of chlorophyll in ours. But Greeks were equally on high alert for degrees of 'chloro', a visual sensation that bore a name that could then be ascribed to emotional states, as Homer did with the expression 'chloros fear'. And as we still do by virtue of habit when we say 'green with envy.' (For a wonderful in depth look at color notions both biological and cultural read *Bright Earth* by Philip Ball.)

One wonders why 'blue' escapes a category of its own, let alone a word of its own until much later in history. The exception was the

Egyptians whose word '*wadjet*' meant a blue-greenish hue. But they celebrated intense blueness in objects with their turquoises and *lapis lazulis*. They synthesized lapis in a dye or tint made of calcium copper silicate, a medium known across the ancient Greco-Roman world with the Romans calling it '*coeruleum*' (our cerulean), and the better-known blue faience found of Egyptian clay objects. It entered the English vocabulary in this descriptive and highly contextual form, and is mentioned in 1809 as 'Egyptian Blue.'

Which logically leads some like Guy Deutscher in his book *'Through the Language Glass; Why the world looks different in other languages'* to suggest that by naming something conditions our perceiving it as a unique category, and vice versa, that not being able to name it mitigates our ability to discern it. This in turn suggests that premodern color ideas were object definitions admixed with the vagary of human feelings, which in turn were matters of context and degrees of comparison. Often, their ideas about color could be a response to the level of the sun and its comparable wavelengths on objects, and their relative ability to reflect or absorb light and own optical ability to discern it.

All color is a reflection of light and the signature wave length bouncing off specific molecules in the objects. This couples with the projection of an individual's sensation and mental mixing of it. The Homeric color of red wine (for they didn't seem to drink or have much in the white wine category), is a value of sliding gradations and not of a single hue. It is predicated on the signature attributes of a specific object rather than a singular, reflected hue. Thus, the color of wine is a composite of thousands of hues and shine bound by the very unique molecular behavior of wine as it reflects a huge range of light quanta in every conceivable forecast. And only red wine color behaves in a characteristic way in dank air or spilled on sand as no other property possibly could. Therefore, all this information belongs to wine, not to milk, and not to red oxide mixed with spit.

*　*　*

Colors are subtle and complex and never pure despite your Photoshop sample. They describe the impending behaviors of all things like the weather and even the change in one's cornea, which can predict mood. They foreshadow behaviors, and we look to them for signals about impending changes to the environment. They are narrative cues because we are always threaded into stories about such and such pending, predicted, or happening. And they are as nuanced as our gestures and verbal language.

They are discreetly infinite too, bounded only by the limitations of our visual physiology just as language is arrayed only by the number of words available and within a construct of syntax and of course, our physical ability to vocalize them.

For the Italian painters of the Renaissance period, mostly notably those trained in the Venetian School like the Bellini family and Titian, tinting was a coloration process of built-up layers of thinly applied glazes or hues. No single, flat color answered the needs of what they saw or what they needed to put across their impression. This was far more accurately observed or 'felt' than what we have today, where color terms indoctrinate or preempt sensitive color perception.

Color does not live only in our optical sensing apparati as all of us innately suspect. Nor can a single word convey enough meaning to evaluate the veridical nature of a given reflected wavelength, which is where color perception begins in our senses. But rather, it comes to us as clustered and conceptualized aggregates, not just through our retina as a mosaic of excited little photoreceptors called cones, but in a far bigger and personalized way about identity as a mercurial but intrinsic description.

Still confused?

Take chartreuse. What does that really look like? Is it a piece of information so distinct that it cannot be subdivided? No. It means a kind of greenish-yellowish or yellow-greenish attribute, especially when it contrasts with black, but not so much when it contrasts with orange-ish.

And on and on. In a Pantone (over 2000 choices and counting) color wheel of greenish yellows, you probably would not be able to point to one hue as epitomizing the word. And certainly not to my choice for it.

You probably also couldn't note the differences in the separated gradations beyond the extreme swings of gradations at either end of the wheel. But 'green' cultures for whom life and death depends on these gradations certainly could, especially tribes like the Himba of Namibia, who have no word for blue. Those hues we so label fall into their green range.

So, while invented words are trying their best to operate in our cognition as something we call morphemes, non-divisible information bytes to expedite life, I suppose then, isn't STROOP saying that we decide ahead of time the terms of our perceiving the world around us?

Here's another fascinating example. Guy Deutscher did not teach his daughter the word 'blue.' Period. He wanted to know how she would describe the color of the sky when she was able to speak. When she did, it was a description of 'white-ness.' A logical thing, since white is as difficult as black to pin down. The scope is that vast. Ask any decent painter who ever tried to paint 'snow' like John Henry Twachtman. Cut out a little square from black or white paper and move it around his painted snow—violets, blues, beige, pinks.

Surprising, very surprising. But not really if you recall that 'anticipation' is one of the four conversion devices we use to visualize.

Expectations and habit lead the way as a matter of expediency and time conservation in our mental lives.

***

Let's go back to the attentional conflict in our ACC anterior cingulate cortex vis-à-vis creating art, especially drawing from life and apply a kind of STROOP test. The brain is being asked to subvert habit or pretext, as in a red apple is an iconic shape/color with the label 'red,' to be executed in real-time terms both as a volume/line/shape presence with many levels of hue and shading. The task is to respond faithfully to the event rather than be guided by a predetermined outcome. Since the task is to check back and forth constantly to both spot and correct errors, there is a significant likelihood of increased amplitude in the error-related negativity response.

It is a constant battle of 'which action rules?' and 'have I just made a mistake?' And a suspicious cognition that neurons fire off around the pretext, 'I might have made an error in execution.' Do we start with the assumptions and rebel against them, contravening the paradigm 'red apple,' or work up from the bottom, adding bit on bit, self-correcting minute step by minute step, and dispensing with any pre-fab directives?

In art, especially life drawing, the conflict is huge. The exertion of mental energy is enormous. Trying to conserve it runs counter to the task at hand to get it 'right' and dispense with convention. Will it either be the belief system that projects the ingrained knowledge as an icon or will it be a jurisdiction of our 'naming' system that is bottom up and goes point to point in motion- induced segments trying hard to build up a valid description?

***

Put another way, which philosophers like Susanna Seigel prefer doing, is to explore the sensory nature of our *'subjective connectedness'* to objects.

> Typical perceptual experiences of seeing ordinary objects present those objects both as independent of the subject and as perceptually connected to the subject. (Seigel 2010)

Our culture is clearly trying its darnedest to expedite perception (to wit, the Verizon commercial, 'It's so thirty seconds ago'). We don't want to be too connected, do we? It just takes too much time and energy. But we still have to know about things, be perceptually connected in some way but able to move on with spryness. We strike a deal. Look at how we fine-tune perceiving and conveying color. 'Subjective connectedness' to *color* is a bit more rarefied a concept than the *object* identification Seigel exclusively refers to. She should have considered this enormous context.

Anyway, enter the handy label.

Labeling expedites communication, and of course just life generally. Nevertheless, the fact is that color recognition is still highly subjective, invented, and rather mercurial. Scientists ask all the time if we have come to standardize visualization routines, and whether this trait is a core significance for our higher level of cognition.

More germane to this discussion is how does the activity of image-creation enact imitations of color perceptions? What is under scrutiny, both in this discussion and in references above and to follow, is an implicit notion of imitative behavior that connects a subject such as you or me with the perception of an independent object, as already stated. As you can see, philosophers and scientists parse the nuances with erudition that exceeds my own, so let me cut to the chase. Is visualization *de rigueur* a wholly predatory action that cannibalizes the independence of any freestanding object because it must be processed by me and in my own way by means of what others have taught about doing things?

Like Seigel's term 'subjective connectedness', Zolton Jakab offers yet another one. His version is often referred to as 'projectivist sensory experience' (Jakab 2003, 2003B), where the subject projects a 'preference,' sometimes more than you think and in variable ways. Simon Baron-Cohen's is similar and worthy of note.

> Far from being a physical property of objects, color is a mental property—a useful invention that specialized circuitry computes in our minds and then 'projects onto' our percepts of physically colorless objects. (Baron-Cohen 1995:xi)

Again, for ancient Greeks, 'wine' as a color could mean the sea, but so could sheep mean the same color. Sheep you say? Ridiculous. But consider that the likelihood is that at dusk, the shadow cast by these all-important protein sources had the same 'feel' (Ings 2007). Observing every appearance of them at all hours, and in all terrain, was essential to survival. A compendium of their colors and forms was a remembered lexicon just as a sailor sees the identity of microwave patterns as prominently as we see highway signs.

For the Greeks, sheep were seen and most importantly counted in the twilight, and looked the same as the deep, inky black sea did. This is my take on the matter, but valid because the emotional content of seeing these objects in fading light, I would imagine, also had certain equivalencies about sustaining life and this had emotional influence too.

And just as an irresistible aside, when an artist wants to get the blackest of all blacks, he mixes Alizaron Crimson into it. It makes the black luminous. Intense darkness being luminous, you say? Now that should really throw a wrench in the works.

Let me just continue a bit longer about color evaluation because it has everything to do with the curious give and take of thinking through color to some degree or other as a previously mentalized predisposition. Visual information is all about intention and anticipation. I think Peter Tse's description of how humans visually 'complete' volumes in space can be applied to visualizing in general. For example, despite so many (Livingstone 2008) insisting that we see in 3D, we just flat out don't. We invent it.

> How is the percept of a 3-D scene constructed from the 2-D retinal image projection? Because many states of the world could project to the same image, the image is inherently ambiguous. To overcome this ambiguity the visual system must make assumptions about the relationship between image information and the structure of the world, and it must infer or 'add' information about the world that is "missing" from the image. (Tse 1999:37)

It's a dialogue of prompts and biased answers. Which brings us back to doodling. It trips search alarms in the same way that the jumbled faze of reality, as in ancient forests and jungle foliage, savannahs, and ice sheets, rock walls, stone crannies and water had to have done too. Finding the important signs in a jumbled mess or in a vast unbroken mass of sameness is not that hard if you have been good at practicing the means by which you convert an object or significance of any kind into meaningful components. As a contrast, autists, demarcate their components very differently than others which is why their responses to cues are also different in many ways.

Elaboration

Throughout this discussion, I have called 'art' a form of exercise for looping meaningful narratives by way of visual components. This is also called long-term memory 'elaboration,' a way of practicing to remember forever. We all do this in clumps of meaningful links or parenthetical groupings. We glue the components by means of specific arrangements that sweep up the concomitant mix of feelings and narrative. This way we don't have to repeat a word constantly or remember an object whole like a blinking neon sign in our head. Sometimes the effort is intentional and sometimes it is just as a matter of course.

For me, the 'doodling' we initially mentioned is a window into the system we use called long-term memory elaboration. Finding the shapes in the scribble is the doodling I have in mind rather than drawing little cartoon characters on the margins of one's note pad. The loops and lines that seem random and a total mess reveal the elaboration itself deconstructed like a film in rewind.

Backward through the components we go. Only certain combinations work and remind us of deeply embedded, long-term imagery. We demarcate the links and highlight them because something about that shape or line element has already tripped a search alarm.

For me, it can even start with an odd, darkish mass on a seemingly perfect white surface like a plain piece of paper. But mass, I have learned over time, implies suggestions about contour, form, and identity. Doodling is a dialogue and much _more_ direct and revealing because I construct freestanding imagery from bare-boned syntax. Yes, pure cognitive syntax that some shape and line linked with something else belong to the attributes of a larger entity. For example, the reddish crack on a cave wall is curved and horizontal just exactly like the underbelly of an ox. Therefore, why not use this as my first 'stroke?' Given that it's a dialogue, selecting the first element or stroke constitutes the salutation directed toward something very specific. It's like saying, 'Hi there, do I know you?' and soliciting an answer.

Yet the 'answer' - the stone-age creator's decisive response to the prompt - still rests on a mentalized imitation of 'ox' (the extinct auroch), which then guides the additive steps that follow. As already mentioned, some scientists like Stephen Kosslyn and Alan Baddeley have worked hard to reason how we do this. They have broken the working memory process and brain elements down to a fairly hierarchical mapping of designated tasks. What they would say about that ultimate concept of an ox resides in an 'episodic buffer,' a coalition of meaningful, related imagery from an individual's life that has been ramped up from a step below called the visual buffer.

This little waystation for imagery coalesces whatever I have visualized in short-term memory that I have rehearsed enough times over in two-second cycles alongside some kind of spatial relating. I have stashed the perception of say 'trees' by parking it briefly in my working memory because I am thinking about it more than just letting it seep out or be replaced by other ideas. This is my visual cache, but it lacks heft if I need to replicate or archive it because I need to add the concept of space and sequence to really nail the image into place.

According to these gentlemen, this requires a slavish 'scribe' or active 'decider' that requires a spatial sequencing. This means the tree in question is number three in a line and looks to be a little behind the fourth. A little amodal brain teasing as it were and a lot of thinking that the world is a big complicate place and that what we see is just the tip of the iceberg. An iceberg by whose behavior we believe we are quite familiar. It also requires an understanding of my own movements to acquire these ideas just as during sketching. It's my environmental context adjuster, the format we use to liken it to how we normally perceive volume and placement. Whether there are a few more or far more steps that the so-called visual buffer combines into an idea of trees in the foreground rather than just trees as a symbol remains to be seen. But the general takeaway is that this is largely an executive function of the prefrontal lobe.

**

Only there is that darn problem about non-stasis mentalizing, a terrible term for which I would welcome a better one. Every time I refer to the abeyant goal, the image I tried to park in my working memory, it has either changed or my efforts to recall it or the ideation is so utterly global, as already mentioned, that we have not got the cognitive strength of mind to zoom in on the local parts. In many respects, it's like Augustine's effort in his '*Confessions*' to explain an idea he has for the concept of time. That he pretty much knows what it is until he has to convert the idea into precise words to communicate it. 'If no one asks me, I think I know what it is. If I try to explain it to an enquirer, I am baffled.' (Armesto 2015:20)

No one really speaks in depth about this conundrum namely, the belief that imagination and working memory seem to be far more detailed than they could possibly be, and that it really can stand up against further scrutiny. This means that has to be a belief that you can return to it, zoom in for details, look around and exit, which of course you cannot. These 'working ideas,' like the foot I am trying to draw or the face that is emerging from the doodles, have a persistence to them, allowing them to be placed in a shallow archive yet totaling lacking a visual scribe. They are significant for being part of a theoretical dilemma still lacking any good answers.

Thus far, Alan Baddeley, the inventor of working memory systems only speaks of the mechanics of recall and of the timing of recall rather than the complex nature of the ideation itself.

There is an enormous confusion inherent in mentalized imagery of any kind—illusions, hallucinations, dreams, and imagined images. One might even suggest that every image is invented but in different ways. Pure non-optic derived images range from divining what color paint would look best on your house as you broadly think about the house either by looking directly at it or in any other manner of imagining. Or remembering the last smile your mother gave you. Or watching yourself at age 16 chase a beam of light from different angles.

In that moment when you are divining the new color for the house, you are really not looking at the façade any more. The quanta are not being sorted in the visual one system. They are being interfered and obstructed. These are all what I call 'global' ideas. The image is in very low resolution, and short-term memory instantly tries to encroach within seconds to replace the perception with a real time visual. There is far less interference when replacing an object memory with a motion memory because the neural pathways are different, the former being in the dorsal stream the latter in the ventral. But for some like Einstein, the constant replacement of the imagic memory with a new one is what one calls 'retroactive memory'. In Einstein's case, we are all very very grateful for that.

***

In short-term (STM) memory speak, this slippery lapsing of a big operative idea like imagining your hideous house bathed in fresh new paint, is called 'retroactive interference'. It is a sequential juggernaut that pushes out or aside the former idea no matter how one might want to rehearse it over and over in the head. In my 'artistic' case, the reason is the recruiting of other sensory motor needs to render into plastic form a different kind of perception—the act of conversion itself. It is the new version of a moment's old idea being formed with the hand as I watch the marks flowing from it. A video clip being edited in real-time.

Calling back the 'Big Idea' to anchor it all is terribly difficult and intrudes on the present short-term recall. Doing this successfully is called 'proactive' interference. This especially happens when I refer to the model before me by looking back at it. Interestingly, no task shifting between two ideas in like visual streams roils everyone's visual cache, suggesting that some emphatic executive function must be making big big decisions about switching things up. One of the decisions might favor short-term memory paradigms or a decision that reaches deeper into long-term memory. This kind of decision-making has not been identified, nor the frustrations that likely produce a fair amount of EEG tracing of the interference itself.

Interference also happens when I try to remember an original inspiration or anything significant in my mental repertoire. Natural beta oscillations of neurons firing and replenishing likely has a great deal to do with this eclipsing of imagery and the need to constantly re-up it if I want to keep it online in my head. Sometimes I get the feeling that a natural neural respiration, a kind of timed erasure, is bearing down on my thoughts.

Defying the natural erasure rhythms of neurons takes some serious determination and elaboration. All neurons need to refresh just like the cones in your eyes. Refreshing causes a momentary enervation and inhibition which causes a problem with retrieval. Although it's a bit of a Catch-22 because the origination of the key, trigger, prompt, prime that permits us to chunk something meaningful for retrieval requires a mnemonic association of it in the first place. How do you associate an idea without the idea? It's a chicken and egg kind of dynamic, like retrieving a book in the library; you have the location coordinates and concept of the book first before heading to the right stack to find it. The idea is embedded in a different part of the brain (i.e., the stacks) than the image pathways I use to bring it forth (i.e., call numbers and subject headings).

***

Einstein famously thought or imagined in pictures, often saying he played the image from all angles to 'see' how it worked before proofing it. He kept it purely mental like playing back a memory of an event or video clip, changing it a bit each time. There might have been a fair amount of interference for him to have done so since the motion and spatial thinking pushed up against each other in the same occipital V1 ventral stream. The likelihood is with each pass the same neurons were needed to execute the continuous refinement of the motion clips in his head and slowed down the processing of his theory... just a bit.

But this is not quite the same thing as I am discussing. I am addressing reverting back and forth between the imagined to the physical activity of copying it down, which involves rehearsing the idea long enough to sustain and then convert it. It is not a memory to be filed in the frontal cortex. It belongs to the 'working memory' system, which is diffuse but has those built-in periodic erasures in the form of oscillations, or neural pulsing of cell assemblies. These occur at the gamma level of over 24 Hz to 60 Hz in the occipital and at the beta level, which is just below that in the frontal lobe (see Tallon-Baudry et al 1999). The brief holding of these images at the onset of the induced stimulus constitutes visual short-term memory, a very brief period during which that memory is delayed before replacing it with a new one.

But with a caveat.

It's like the old Greek parable by way of Heraclitus that says, 'No man ever steps into the same river twice.' No matter how stimulating the visual idea might be and no matter how hard you try to rehearse it to carve out a place for it in your working memory and then on to long-term memory, the fact is that inevitable replacement of a stimulus is too overwhelming, as already mentioned. The fluidity of thought and the context of your environment constantly alters the train of your thinking. You might try to 'chunk' your visual memory to hold the contents with a kind of riddle or mini-narrative as I often practice. But long-term, my mother's smile inevitably fades over time.

For example, I can remember faces rather well, once and done. I can't resurrect them, but I can recognize them should they pass my way again. Not because I am particularly gifted, but because I allow my opinion to jump forward about every person I see. This includes their clothing, odd walks, nice shoes, any oddity. And every person has something that *is* a bit quirky to your mind if you invest a moment to define them. Everyone's face is part of a built-in, and I dare say, gossipy, maybe even snarky little narrative. We need to accept that one of the reasons we have endured is what politically correct activists are trying so hard to control. We are catty and suppressing it will just make it erupt anyway.

Prosopagnosiacs should give this gossipy even snarky - approach a try. Look at a face and say or think something critical of it. Simultaneously prick or bend your index finger, the outlining and volume radar we all have. It works like a charm as far as rudimentary passive recognition goes; the face links as a caricature. One cannot forget it now. One can format the face into clumps along preconceived notions that are based on your personal and deeply trained memory cache: 'That nose she has looks like Nefertiti's, no more like Uncle Moe's but with a little bump at the bridge shaped like the Rock of Gibraltar.'

Art rarely achieves a reference for this kind of high-profile chunking. On the rare occasions when becomes axiomatic it is called iconic. And as with anything iconic, a memorable story accompanies it. Instead, art reaches for low-profile chunking or else no one would bother creating. It is a personal kind of reference that we all would hope becomes a universal but rarely can. These are the recognition and search paradigms I have already addressed. However, along the way, if the story along the way becomes big and notorious then the whole package somehow gets advertised sufficiently and we get a 'Mona Lisa'.

Given the iconic power of Nefertiti's nose, it still gets complicated. If you cleverly reference her nose, you might get caught up in her face rather than the one in front of you and lose the idea of her bump. Switching between the memory of Nefertiti's nose and the memory of that someone else's bump confuses the present ideation. They invoke the same cells and make the short-term memory of it much shorter than had you listened to a song while trying to remember her features.

To recall non-iconic faces, we tend to scoop up the features and remember the whole fuzzy face idea, which is short-lived beyond a maximum capacity of 18 seconds. Still, there are certain details that predominate. Scientists Steven Luck and Edward Vogel believe that 3 to 4 objects, regardless of the features contained within, are the upward limit of short-term visual memory. The implication being that short-term memory, the intake capacitor for working memory and on, is an object filter rather than an abstraction filter. I have to add that for artists, the process of depiction makes objects of abstract details like shadows and line subtleties. When drawing, for example, short-term memory converts abstractions into objects like the bumpy contour of a nose bridge. The Luck-Vogel idea of object cohesiveness for VSTM might need further testing because abstractions are always objects but without names.

Seeing is hard. Very very hard. 'Art' is hard because conversion is harder. Let's take another look at mirroring, the fourth conversion device.

Mirroring is tough sledding but it results in a form of symmetry. The mental rigors of undertaking the concept of symmetry suggests a cognitive sophistication never directly addressed in detail in Paleoanthropology. The earliest known knapping of a biface chopper found in Gona, Ethiopia was brilliant stuff and not the exclusive domain of our species. Rather it arrived with the smaller brains of 2.6 million years before us (Olduwan, possibly Australopithecus or Homo Habilis, Ergaster, or other), who had a fabric of neurons and the right kind to sustain the activity.

Sustaining the activity is essential here. Literally, the notion of following through on a unique activity for a bit of time. Sustaining it can be very dicey and this is why our distant cousins deserve a lot more kudos for their gargantuan efforts. The reason is that since we are motor creatures we basically can't stop moving. Therefore, we are always switching gears, especially when we fabricate objects.

The visual short-term memory cannot be sustained long enough to be of much continuous help; it's a river flowing and we keep moving and scanning the visual field. We keep checking back and back and back, object, hand, head, etc. This casts a few doubts on recent findings for their timed capacity of VSTM. Eighteen seconds is an eternity, and our brains hate stasis, repetitions, and sustained ideas. We really must ensure that experiments mimic our real visual realities. Not just static lab behaviors.

Why was it easier for Einstein to imagine from various angles and behaviors? First, it's not easy to do this, but some rare folk like Einstein and Temple Grandin, among many others, could keep visualizations intact by continually changing the thinking, the angles, the speed of the film played in his head, and the narrative of who and how a beam of light was being chased. Two reasons; In order to replay the scene in a new way the Great One shifted the emphasis between object and motion among other things.

And the other thing was by making the whole mental event into a story and by doing so, shifting his VSTM to a long-term niche. Consequently, he came close to stepping into the same memory many times over, just from different entry doors, so to speak. It's like shooting a scene with several cameras running simultaneously. The raw footage can film action and stasis. That footage can then be run backward, repeated, and intercut in the editing. When stitched together, it requires the viewer to play along with a four-dimensional belief: space/time along with the three dimensions of length, depth (i.e., width), and height. What is interesting about these comments he made over time, is that they appear to be consistently motion or dorsal ideas rather than static or ventral ones. They weren't though. It's a thankless job second guessing Einstein but there is simply no way to loop a mental story about a person moving let alone a ray of light unless the first frame or two is a static image of the object itself with many others strewn about.

CONVERSION DEVICES

PART FOUR

Novelty

Either way, what we imagine, even what we see in front of us can never be the image we draw. Nor the image we draw on. When I draw, I can feel that visualizing on different terms such as memory to page and back creates a bottleneck. That bottleneck is in the storage and rehearsal effort that is being interrupted, intervened, displaced, and contravened because I am recruiting the same neurons for conflicting stimuli.

> One crucial research question in this field is how maintenance of information in working memory is still accomplished when interference impedes rehearsal mechanisms to keep information online. (Kessler and Kiefer 2004)

Why the conflict? Common sense suggests that the same neurons are being used to store an image and/or visuospatial image so that a glance at a figure creates a short-term memory of an object that is displaced by a glance at the paper or fabrication underway. 'The standard result is that combining two tasks of the same type causes lower memory performances than combining two tasks of different types' (Zimmer 2008). Or as everyday driving a car with chattering kid's parlance goes, 'Stop it. Only one at a time. I can't understand both of you.' Researchers believe that the visual spatial cache tends to be corrupted by the sameness of the motion or sequence of movements.

Does art even try to keep information online? Because in essence, I am correcting the original image with a sequence of movements. This is also a spatial task just as my observation of the live model is in real-time space. Some researchers believe that these spatial neurons are like-minded. I don't, but that's another story.

During life drawing, my task is bold and simple - to account for errors during image-fabrication as it compares to the controls in my visualization system which I trust to be more reliable. But as I correct the so-called errors from my transcribing I am in essence changing the working memory of the 'idea' in my head. These regions of greatest cerebral interest are the Anterior Cingulate Cortex, the Dorso Lateral Prefrontal cortex, and the Medial Temporal lobe.

***

Nothing resultant from inspiration ever delivers a clone of its initial idea. The act of fabrication so dilutes and obfuscates the originating precept that the first goal that responds to your prompts soon becomes a mix of the physical product in front of you and a shadow of the original idea. Often, when we speak of 'inspiration,' what we are really saying is that randomness in living and the environment triggers a previously cast synchronization of neurons like tripping an alarm, 'It's *déjà vu* all over again.'

In this sense, inspiration draws on familiarities living in our long-term memory. Art marshals these connections into a single event, which in turn confirms and incises the connections deeper into LTM. If this were not true, then why even in the most high-end galleries do they still show 'objects' as we have always done. Everyday ones like ice cream cones (plastic), tilted chairs, etc. with more and more a dependency on photography to support graphic design and painting.

Our tendencies remain the same i.e., to practice recognition with narrative influence to solidify the long-term memory for it. The exercise is far more effective when it is a summation of many sensory modalities, and highly kinesthetic at that. We walk around, touch, see, perceive volumes, sense time and distance from object such that it allows us to loop various video 'footage' of the art event. In essence, art in any potential, whether just experiencing it or making it, is a slice of living. It is motile in our brains and engages both the rather obvious occipital ventral and dorsal streams. And like Einstein's thought experiment, it allows us to enter and reenter from all angles and from different times. And most significantly, to change the attributes.

**

Even today, many reputable scientists still cling to the dogma that 'image-making' is lateralized for right-brain dominance and that artists can't read fast. Or that because of this lopsidedness, '...reading fluency and artistic ability have, in my experience, been mutually exclusive' (Livingstone 2008:199). Had they been artists themselves, they would never have said such a silly thing, which is now thankfully a highly challenged theory. Add to that the fact that 'artistic ability' is an incredibly empty term and virtually useless in a scientific discussion.

Their general reasoning is that symbolism from which letter representation to word and concept configuration is contrived - or derives -is a left-dominant piece of real estate known as Broca's Area. This too is a remarkably superficial understanding of image-crafting, or perhaps even more worrisome, what an 'image' is. The most obvious retort being that most of the human record has been analphabetic, and that 'reading' imagery as in story-boarding narratives, whether on murals, oil paintings, a single piece of statuary, vases, comic books, church lintels or carvings, is also symbolic syntax construction.

Therefore, we invite the reader to consider that 'imitation' as a transcription process onto stable media is far more complex and laterally egalitarian. Scientists should spend more time on this process as it brings into keener focus the degree and development of iconographic attributes. Most interestingly is how they are grouped, triaged and tweaked over the lifetime of an individual. Because our imitative strategies, the way we map out these behaviors changes drastically over time.

***

When speaking of 'imitation' we immediately think of aping a gesture and sound or snapping a photo and trying to draw realistically. When it comes to imitating behavior and cultural copying, we call this 'emulation' (Tomasello 1999; Clayton, Dugatkin 2010; Holldobler 2010; Hauber 2010), its offshoots being trends or fads. The longer lasting ones that propagate widely become what some call 'memes,' a persistent snippet of cultural traditions that get passed along like a gene and are subject to mutation. This means they can morph from the original fad. Such macro-behavioral emulation reverberates on a micro-behavioral and neural level that conforms our brain to copying habits that are remarkably automatic. Habits that format our ability to transfer these inner-emulation strategies to external media.

This investigation suggests that some survival behaviors mediate our impulse for externalizing imitation strategies into freestanding notations. Merlin Donald, the psychologist/anthropologist, has called these notations 'external symbolic storage,' versions of which I am very very loosely calling 'art.'

> Meaningful marks are being made upon some object so that their meanings can be revisited at a later date...'
> (Renfrew 2009:77)

But what catalyzes the impulse to craft them in the first place, let alone convert them from brain to hand? Prominent among these 'conversion devices' is how we, like most creatures, are designed to scan the world for 'novelty.' We need to store information coherently and differently so that 'novel' information is available for speedy retrieval. This most definitely includes 'external symbolic storage,' like those storyboards on Medieval church lintels, vases, Australian rock art, comics, cave art, etc. Or the rough depiction of a fish with huge, bulging eyes.

How do we make the determination for what is novel and worth externalizing? As with everything else in our lives, we do it by effectively designing baselines and deviations around them.

Our primary motivation in all aspects of living is to prognosticate environmental behaviors. This includes the intangible and tangible messaging of the environment that we can intercede to formulate our most successful survival outcomes. We're talking 'speed' here. Recognition tricks enhance the speed. If you think about it, the word 'recognition' means to re-up an existing judgment, or to 're-cognitize' it. This doesn't mean to just 'loop' as in to rehearse and rehearse it mechanically without an urgent pretext. Such a goalless habit dulls our brains like a constant and steady mono-decibel beat. Who cares to remember that phone number for the lumberyard beyond the time it took to dial it? No, 're-cognition' means to keep it present and active by 're-thinking' about it in meaningful ways.

Recognition is highly imitative on several levels. First, there must be a preexisting design, the thing itself, and second, we like to imitate it by slipping real-time prompts into their shadow paradigms. Think of how you can opt to 'unlock' your Droid phone by sliding an icon puzzle piece into its phantom slot, or a key into a lock. Well, recognition ironically depends on discerning what is novel rather than what is familiar. It depends on rapidly 'unlocking' what is significant from the ambient neural noise of pervasive synaptic firings.

Here's an aside: If you figure that, on average, a synapse fires 300 to 1000 times per second, and we have from 60 to 100 trillion of these, but much of it is enervated or suppressed, we still get a number that is frightening, noisy, and big. To unlock salient imagery from all the neural noise requires some kind of resident shadowy imagery. We cannot determine if it is salient and worthwhile unless we measure it against what is not.

***

What is divorced from science and anthropology research is the thunder of human emotional power. The sands yield dry silent bones; the synapses yield electrical oscillations. But it is our emotional palette that colors our intentions for just about everything we have rendered in habit and hearsay since our ten toes dug deep into the loam to walk us out of danger; adrenaline, fear, happiness, desperation, relief, curiosity.

We've already mentioned how our scientific literature is rife with the notion of recognition templates, typologies, paradigms etc. The problem with all of this is that it addresses these designs as a *'fait accompli'* rather than how it gets physiologically seared into our brains in the first place.

Humans, as with most animals, abhor being shocked. (When was the last time you were?) We enjoy the thrill as long as it's in a controlled outcome like a horror film, story, or newspaper, or 'haunted house ride.' But in everyday living, our species has evolved with signature coping devices that also help to deflate it. These are the biological and cognitive mechanisms that we employ to scan for novelty.

'Novelty' derives from an evolutionary imperative for survival. It is not for nothing that our eyes jump or saccade at least three times a minute seeking, looking, briefly fixating, and moving on (Purves 2008; Ings 2007; Ungerleider 1998; Hsieh 2010). Or that when fixating, we are not designed to rest our fovea on a concentrated unit for more than a fraction of a second or we 'blank out.' An aspect of this is called perceptual fading or the Toxler Effect, discovered in 1804 (Wyder 2004; Purves 2008), when an object, '...remains stabilized upon the retina as happens under conditions of visual fixation' (Hsieh 2010:1).

These eyes of ours were designed to be restless because our brains are. They are designed to seek novelty and build up information about the content of the environment by aggregating an endless stream of information about it, around it, and near it to maximize thinking. Because we are de jure the questing animal, we need to know what can be discounted and not worth attention because it is regular, recurring, and known. Versus anomalies that require considerable focus. Constantly 'scanning' for novelty might sound counterintuitive, even masochistic and certainly compulsive. But we do it because, as already stated, we hate being caught unaware.

***

Of course, one needs to be careful assigning a singular driver for this behavior such as a summa-amygdalic alternator that automatically normalizes emotional peaks and troughs. This doesn't mean something in our limbic system that dulls our fear and flight reflexes. It means something in our prefrontal cortex that necessarily distracts and overrides it. We do this all the time.

*

It is not for nothing that our closest genetic cousin, the 'chimp,' has a nervous system that abhors inactivity. Desmond Morris famously suggested (Loizos 2006) that chimps are 'specialists in non-specialization,' or opportunists with a raging 'neophilia' or love of the new. Sounds like your typical teen. Or many of us with the latest smartphone and addiction to checking messages and getting new info bytes by the minute if not second.

Some primatologists have determined that heterogeneity for chimps is stimulating. Well, it is for us too. Recall a few pages back the revelation that we are a necessarily catty species. We can't help noticing the novelty of each face in real time. But in a much broader way one might wonder if perhaps this has always been our stock in trade?

Consider the vast distances we have trekked over time and even now with the swarms of refugees on every continent; barefoot, exhausted, hungry and cold, to say the least and never certain of the destination nor what to expect along the way. Remove the exigency of the crisis and you still get the restlessness as the sculptor Louise Nevelson and so many others have quipped about death; it's about always moving forward until you can't anymore.

Are we phylogenetically just a highly strung out and neurotic clade, or is 'novelty' a survival tactic acquired, learned, taught, and passed down, which has served us magnificently well? Might our reflex for constantly scanning with our eyes and rushing through thoughts that jump here and associate there all be linked with a mandate of our species to establish baselines against credible threats and untoward deviations? If you could just sit and capture how many mini-thoughts sweep through your head in ten seconds, you'd have to hope this behavior had some useful purpose. And as for 'seeing,' I know it doesn't appear to you to be forced and exhausting, but take a rare moment to attentively watch yourself doing it. Notice the movement of your eyes, the nature of the way your eyes jump or saccade, and why you move them here or there.

Why *do* you move them here and there? Well, try not moving them. How do you even know where to move them? Do you just plain old know something your eyes don't? Maybe something you caught from the corner of a previous glance for which you needed a second look? If you try not to and willfully fixate on a small point, in split seconds you will no longer see clearly, let alone think clearly. Your concentration on the focal point is entirely subverted. Your thinking about it is thoroughly exhausted, more like fuzzy.

It's as if we need to collect information around a point of interest rather than the point itself. Or put another way, a point of interest is really not a point, but a collection of noteworthy, minute attributes. A grab bag, a cluster, a grouping of small identifiers. On a more macro scale, if you intentionally look out for something, you'll miss something else, or if you are distracted by something, you miss the activity going on around it. If you are shown a picture with a primary focal point, you'll miss the smaller changes around it when asked to look at it altered. We don't need a named experiment to prove it. Who doesn't already know all this?

Then notice that between saccadic sweeps, you are functionally blind. Well, you couldn't really notice that because your intention is so purely anticipatory. But you might realize that:

> Voluntary goal directed saccadic eye movements engage broadly distributed neural network.... A critical function of processing within this network is to ensure that gaze shifts are both timely and appropriate...(they) are not random and choices of where to look are informed both by extrinsic factors, such as the inherent salience of stimuli that compose the visual scene and intrinsic factors, including expectation, motivation and anticipated outcome. (Wyder 2004)

Self-observation of your eye fixations will exhaust you with the thinking it involves. What it will do is make you aware of the fact that we cannot attentively seek novelty *all the time*. Not only would that dull the contrast potential of it, but it would blunt the impact. Constant alerts are just as numbing as being alert constantly. Instead, we seek its kissin' cousin, a baseline of normal against which something unusual is stentorian.

Baseline Patterns

The most autodidactic model for the concept of all baselines is logically the imitation of our own physical self. It seems to be incipient, both already formed yet receptive to more forming. We know this through and through, both implicitly and explicitly, over time. Our bilateralism reverberates a symmetric incumbency that is so latent that infant perception and self-awareness learning, as in limb extension and mimicking caregivers, quickly makes this basic pattern redundant. It becomes a stealth operative of perfection that is semantic, unconscious, and automatic. In other words, very early on, we establish a sense of symmetry as a baseline and treat as novelty that which defies this balance.

For example, our created record continually punctuates this seeming dichotomy. Symmetry is a mirrored repeat pattern. But we welcome all repeat patterns and cover small items with them as much as vast living expanses - such as architectural motifs like the Yeseria plaster work of the Alhambra in Granada, Spain (fig. 10). But look at the way your local provender arranges cans on a shelf. In all of this, there is an implicit bilateralism or symmetry (Filler 2007; Lynch 2008; Wade 2006) that draws us to the mirroring of our own bodies, something in which we find great comfort because it is so familiar. One half of our body mirrors the other. In Photoshop parlance, this is called 'flip horizontal.' Compare this phenomenon to the isolated imagery or icons we often attribute to 'fine art,' wherein singular imagery takes a central position, thus signaling that more attention is required.

***

Let's take a moment and go a bit further with the notion of symmetry and repeat arrangements because they are deeply evocative of how we emotionalize our surroundings and what survival cues we practice from them.

For example, symmetry also implies regular, periodic arrangements like arrays, fractals, tiling, rotary designs, reflections, or generalized and inferred repeats. Inferred repeats are fascinating as brain teasers because they are not true repeats nor truly symmetrical. This is especially prominent in African (i.e., Kuba) textile design (Adams 1989) and Japanese and Roman mosaic designs in which the general form seems fairly regular though the individual elements are unique.

We shouldn't be too surprised by our disposition to gloss over the inconsistencies. Slice a grapefruit and you get what appears to be a general radial repeat of wedge shapes that vary considerably in contour. The macro-pattern represses the micro-variations. In our search for novelty we quickly gloss over the typicality of patterns even when they are not pure repeats because there is not enough obvious aberration contained therein.

It is our cognitive and emotional predisposition to regularity and seeking baselines that chooses to dismiss the minor fluctuations. Anticipation and novelty are conversion devices that always go hand in hand. Nature shows us all this as in crystal formations, in both their macro and molecular constructions, in marine protozoa, in the wings of flies, wasp nests, the overall gross repeat of ripples in sand dunes, though they are completely non-identical as we all know. Imagine the time sink invested in looking for the needle in the haystack or identical pebbles along a stream bed. We have to make assumptions to get on with living.

Obsessive compulsive behavior might welcome this kind of perfection seeking as a quieting diversion from the stress of life, but most of us simply haven't the time to focus on the minutiae. So, we formulate a sweeping concept for the overall impression of these out of kilter patterns and minor fluctuations.

We quickly perceive that our own bilateralism is forward-oriented, that there is a back and front, a dorso ventral-ity to almost everything. (Consider Goethe's original and highly disputed theory of a universal archetypal bilateralism which was later proven with the homeobox gene. See Kuratani 2005). Oddly, when there isn't any perceived frontal bilateralism it suggests that something must be significantly wrong or about to become so. Within that seeming equanimity and balance, there is a reliable dis-equanimity signal.

Artists feast on this contrast. Often what we call 'fine art' is calling attention to what fractures or disquiets the baseline while we assign 'decoration' to the realm of establishing the baselines, the repeats, the calming, acceptable non-jarring, and therefore non-provocative imagery. I don't.

***

Mimicry also reenacts right-left handedness (Bainbridge 2008; Filler 2007; Cavanagh 2008), not just by means of our own dominant 'handedness' which tends to be right sided, but also as we assimilate the same tendencies in nature. Or maybe that we just seem to look for it more. Most vines and animal horns twist right and so does our cerebral cortex. But who could have naturally noticed that! Further we come to know that our favorite primitive design as in the spiral and its 3D version, the helix, can perform a kind of acrobatic miracle. They can dilate and grow in size without changing the shape and angles of the curves. This is known as a logarithmic spiral or *spira mirabilis*. Nature has demonstrated this phenomenon in mollusk shells and galaxy formations and a whole lot in between.

Those marvelous spirals that we all scribble on the margins of our notebooks and whatnot, can reverse and double back on each other, as in the famous labyrinth and earliest formal engravings throughout the late Mesolithic (ca 10,000 to 6,000 BC) and Neolithic.

These graphics are best known from the carvings found in the pass-through graves of Ireland, along the Atlantic coast of France and the Iberian Peninsula. Knowth and Newgrange in Ireland and Gavrinis in Brittany are well known but not the earliest examples. What's particularly interesting about the spiral design is that it appears in mirrored or repeating formations and is famously mankind's go-to decorative motif which emerged out of a long and rather unexplained artistic dry spell.

It is present on the carved pillars of Gobekli Tepe in Turkey that date as far back as 12 millennia to what some might call the Epi-Paleolithic. The Maltese islands in the Mediterranean also sport these spirals, which are guessed to be as old as seven millennia. Curiously, the spirals are not present in the far more sophisticated Upper-Paleolithic iconography of the famous cave paintings. These preceded the Turkish and Maltese lithic structures by several thousand years, which in turn preceded Gavrinis, Newgrange and others along the Atlantic seaboard. All of which prominently employ the helical motif.

To what end - we really don't know, other than the happy discovery of a unique form resulting from a continuous going around and around in the dirt. It is the track of a circle that is dragged across a format. Concentric circles require lifting the stylus and replacing it. A vortex doesn't. Just put down your marker and let it rip. It is a motion induced form with so many variations based on the movement of your stylus. If you draw a circle and move while doing so, the shape becomes a repeat of loops, a flattened double helix. If you widen your arm reach as you do it, then you have a labyrinth or vortex.

The beauty of the discovery was the ability to mimic the shape over and over, and that others could do so as well. Plus, it feels good doing it. It was a full body and brain event that members of your community could mimic perfectly. It was therefore, a cultural replicator, a learned and copied activity to be passed along. One could say, and I am not willing to be that one, that such an image converts a far-flung, extended family into a culture by means of branding it. Yes, the spiral was a brand like Juicy Couture and the Apple Logo. You knew who you were if you did it, displayed it, drew it, knew it.

This might be why we keep making certain things that look generally the same. They become cultural idioms and propagate across space and time to such extremes as to be seen in Egyptian iconography and far more pointedly in the Paleolithic and Mesolithic, where imagery was so standardized to persist intact for tens of thousands of years and across enormous swathes of terrain. Think about today and how fast we move through cultural trends, best seen in styles or art or architecture. If we were to step away and look at these things with a backward glance, how new would they really be?

Now consider how durable cave art was and how far reaching it was over a period of twenty thousand years. Incredible. How is their cultural iconography so pervasive and durable and ours so mercurial? Think of the megalith circles that peppered Europe throughout the megalithic and early Neolithic, a period that also lasted almost 15,000 years. Then the question that always needs to be answered is why were the forms 'stamped' in stone and probably other media like a cattle brand to begin with?

Why does the labyrinth and double coil always crop up? Why does the sigmoid or reverse curve become the motif *du jour* of so much decoration as in all kinds of branching and sub-branching? You see this in classical but also Maori, Greenland, and Alaskan themes, and on and on, including the latest leg prostheses for amputee soldiers.

The spiral becomes a mad riot of design, associated easily with floral dynamism, but also of serpentine and oceanic/water behaviors. It impresses us with an emphatic global symmetry, even when the local variations are remarkably rogue. Take a good hard look; those cresting waves reflected by sunlight are all different from each other, aren't they?

Now go back and really look hard at the so-called cultural trends we zip through. The media might have changed, but the image bias remains the same. The first abstract paintings retired folks do are zigzags and circles. They are fractals of nature's habits. We all think we have invented something unique. But even the typical paintings younger artists do are combinations of these things with embedded body parts. Defiant graffiti art is a riot of sigma curves and reverse spirals.

The point is that just as in nature, where repetitive behavior of forms and colors is used to advantage, 'the charm lies in the fact that it is repetitive, yet infinitely variable.' Infinite creative enactments of any kind are bounded by the arrangement of these finite available parts that are synonymous with the human perceived environment. If you don't believe this at face value, you might want to consider how many versions of, say, cat images have been produced over the human record. Or faces. Or leaves. Or the 'X' shape. We understand the intent of the artist, though there is a cultural bias that might marginally expedite or delay responsiveness if you are unfamiliar with that culture.

For example, many of us find it difficult at first to glom on to the 'X-ray' drawings of the Australian Paleolithic and Aboriginal North Territory of Arnhem. Eventually we do, but hardly as fast as present-day natives. We also find the 360 perspective of Northwest territory iconography, both from ancient and current Inuits, to be at once perplexing until we dispense with our traditional horizon-based, full-frontalism (White 2003). I admit it takes me a while. Nevertheless, they all have fluid legibility, eventually that is, even though the arrangement and nature of such limited parts are universally varied.

Nature then sets the framework for language, once described by Wilhem Von Humboldt as an 'infinite variety of finite media' (or means). We are talking about internal structure, hierarchical grouping, balance, and relative value. In other words, conceptual fractals. Innate syntax. This is the infinite option for defining by means of redefinition. Or recursion. Recursive structuring, therefore, has inevitability written all over it (pun intended) because all that we know and the context of everything we perceptually seek is underscored by an insistent, rigorous, and semantic order.

Individual exposure over time builds out autobiographical emphasis and style from internal programming for bilateralism, symmetry, and repeats. It is an imitative behavior of such enormous and emphatic persistence that we take it for granted and fail to validate how integrative it is across all manner of sensations and activities. It forms a syntactical basis for our productive lives, including emotional. And across all historical time.

Adverts and Sensitivity

One would think that repeat patterns, therefore, evoke a quiescent and non-challenging presence, whereas unique imitations do not. If the most reliable baseline we know is bilateralism, which repeats through the mirrored versions of our most visible body parts (i.e., hands, feet, fingers, etc), one could extrapolate that consistency as a trigger for feeling 'safe and secure.' But our mind cannot stop being suspicious of intention even when assessing platitudes or safe modes like a nice overall repeat on a chocolate cupcake. It takes a nano-moment to convince us that all is well. But that is after scanning as far and as fast as needed across the pattern and seeking the anomalies until we decide we can walk away. It seems that we unconsciously decide that it is not a worthwhile investment in cognitive and frankly emotional energy.

Perhaps repeat patterns are a neural and behavioral conditioning process that moves short-term memory out of the hippocampus and into the neocortical complex for long-term storage, a ho-hum habituating process that the work of Eric Kandel at Columbia University discovered streamlines synapse connectivity by withering the dendrites (Kandel 2006).

But what of sensitization that physically builds out synapses specifically for triggering immediate responses to threats? Emotion makes memory sticky and so hard to silence. It makes us think in terms of episodes, that a unique event linked to an image is solid and memorable. The amygdala has been found to parse these signals of salience into separate cortical pathways for unconscious and implicit memory, and very upfront, attentive, and explicit recollecting.

***

The difference between the two, implicit versus explicit, might have something to do with the nature of freewill and cognitive decisiveness that Benjamin Libet, after the work of Hans Kornhuber, independently discovered regarding voluntary action and 'readiness potentials.' Libet found that the urge to move a finger was prefigured, on average, at about 250 milliseconds beforehand, and that there is a lapse between decision and awareness.

> ...the brain evidently 'decides' to initiate or, at the least, prepare to initiate the act at a time before there is any reportable subjective awareness that such a decision has taken place. It is concluded that cerebral initiation even of a spontaneous voluntary act, of the kind studied here, can and usually does begin unconsciously. (Libet 1983:640)

More anecdotally, but just as valid, is Michael Land's observation that a cricketer takes his eye off the ball to anticipate where it will bounce, thus providing motor information and planning a good second before the muscular movement is activated. Land would call Libet's 'readiness potentials' a 'buffer zone' of at least a half second, where visual information is 'considered' before awareness decides to activate a response.

Honestly, who doesn't know this about themselves that when walking, we always look at least thirty feet ahead to prefigure what our feet will be doing up to that point, even though we advance our focal point off it almost immediately. If we didn't do this, we'd trip over them and become snarled in the here and now.

*

Technically speaking, we are always spatially functioning in the 'past' but thinking in the future. We have two present moments, the cognitive sensory one and the physiological follow-through, which are discordant. For both, we are mapping or imitating our environment (Istomin 2009; Blaut 1987, 1991; Blaut and Stea 2003). We must to navigate and plan. A facsimile of sorts has to be obtained and managed in our heads. Therefore, we objectify it and ourselves as a moveable dot around and through 'it.' What is really being addressed here is the level of clear and present need to act out on neural imitation responses, something we explore regarding another conversion device called 'mirroring.'

But as it concerns patterns and repeats, I suggest that our vigorous, internal affinity for symmetry and bilateralism unconsciously evaluates the significance of these in our 'buffer zone' by sliding the type of repeat into a preexisting phantom slot. Either it fits and can be discounted, in which case the 'potential' urge to react is dismissed and habituated, or something about it doesn't align with implicit expectations and the 'readiness potential' converts to full awareness and motor response.

***

Evaluating the 'intention' of our environment steps up the urgency for assessing novelty by mixing in the emotional glue secreted as it were by the amygdala. As humans evolved, some comparative cortical developments with our closest genetic cousin, the chimpanzee, outpaced others. Our neocortex, for example, is three times their size (Turner 2008). However, the sub-cortical differences that wire us for emotions and supply the glue for long-term memory compare differently. These are generally a little less than twice as large, with the exception of the amygdala, the emotion generator.

This neural cluster, often referred to as our fight-or-flight sensor, is well over twice the size. Interesting, isn't it? And it is highly significant for stimulating the need to mimic 'intention.' Outputs from the thalamus, the sensory switching station for haptics, motor, visual, and auditory that orchestrates what goes where and how fast, travels a much shorter distance to the amygdala before reaching their respective neocortical lobes.

When discussing how to mediate for 'intention' and 'novelty,' what we really are addressing is the construction of what Maynard Smith described as notifications and adverts about our world (Stegman 2005). By 'notifications,' we mean recurring but generally benign patterns that need not command our full emotional attention in comparison to adverts or alarms that are significant and demand full awareness. Either way, our image-making impulse is our cognitive meta-tool for practicing what is 'enough' information for us to make speedy assessments - that which can be discounted and that which simply cannot be overlooked. 'Alerts' are 'adverts' are 'alarms.'

I'm guessing the proliferation of all these prompts fulfills some biologically driven need I have to compensate for my constantly faltering visualization ability. Let's also remember that eyesight is rarely 20/20. In the United States alone, about 70% wear corrective lenses. Our ancestors likely were prone to myopia, astigmatisms, cataracts, etc. As for our primate brethren, no one as far as I know has tried measuring the vision of the great apes, and if finding it, has tried altering or correcting it with glasses or implants.

Would their behavior change?

Assume that we historically have required and therefore invented bold prompts that poor vision could effectively use. If you factor in that we are the result of peripatetic hominids that quested across unknown terrain and bewildering climes, it becomes easier to understand why survival might depend on the versatility of 'recognition' perception and why humans require assists for its unmitigated redefinition and retooling.

Life History and Imitation Cues

Our life history supports this suspicion because we know that our ability to 'read' the world changes constantly. For example, face learning and recognition ability has been shown to peak in early adulthood (ca 32) and then taper (Germine 2010). Correlating this with life history mating and child rearing imperatives might suggest the deterministic need to tune up recognition (e.g. spot your child in a crowd, fall in love) despite an incredibly wide range for normal. It embraces prosopagnosiacs at one extreme who are severely deficient to super recognizers at the other extreme who never forget a face (Russell 2009).

There are some transitional phases in our lives for which spotting the configuration of a face in a crowd is really the only way to recognize the loved one. It would be difficult to try to look for the deviated septum, left cheek mole, or slightly amblyopic eye in the far distance.

'Recognition sensitivities' is a more politically correct way to say what really motivates us in life (i.e. preferences). Studies are constantly being conducted for age groups with nationalities that demonstrate the transient preferences for face configurations. Which again is a nice way of saying 'good looking.' We respond to what might seem like a mercurial concept of attractiveness, depending on our particular phase of life. Mating seeks a different facial replicator signal than post-pregnancy.

*

How we translate social behaviors as in 'who is a reliable defender and provider' into visualization cues would logically be resultant from a sensitization process that eventually becomes habituated into a baseline pattern. Bolstered by an enormous framework of commingled habits acquired through stories, teaching, communal politics, gossip, and observation, over time still requires an autobiographical kicker that enhances perspicacity.

I contend that this is the secretion of adrenaline from heightened emotions that are survival-dependent.

By necessity, we learn to spot the caricature (Valentine 1991; Giovanelli 2006; Bruce 1986). The general thinking is that we progress naturally in recognition ability toward configured face formation. This means the relationship of features among themselves, as opposed to specific feature recognition - the big nose, the protruding lower lip, etc. - which makes sense, particularly when discussing life history.

And even more so considering the increasing need to read emotions as indicators of potentially positive or adverse effects on the individual. For example, toddlers have been shown to '...correctly identify sad and happy more than any other expression' (Giovannelli 2006:15).

Think about it. Emotions alter facial features. Noses shorten or pull up depending on what the mouth is doing, and thus configurations link directly with emotional legibility. The ability to discriminate subtler emotions further increases with age and tops out at around ten years old when further improvement tapers.

The Teeth of it

But let's back up a moment because life history has a direct bearing on the prejudices of perspectives and how we are disposed to both screen and interpret sensory inputs Point of view has everything to do with how successful communication will be.

Age five (to seven) is extremely significant for dentition with the eruption of permanent central incisors and first molars. Why is it so important? Because in human development, this signifies the ability to eat meat, at which point a child could technically survive on its own. It is also significant developmentally as a time when we become extremely 'explorative' and tend to wander off from the security of a nurturer's firm grip (Wood 1997). Wandering off and being able to eat meat might be highly connected and have 'Theory of Mind' (ToM) implications too (Baron-Cohen 1995; Botha 2010). Because also occurring around this age (4 to 5 years), experiments have shown that a sensitivity for what is called 'False Beliefs' in others has kicked in.

It is a transitional phase during which a commonality of perspectives (i.e., the projection of 'self' as the observed actor) begins to frame perception with standardizations, stereotypes, and prejudgments. These insinuate themselves as teachable, cultural identities by means of myths, rhymes, icons, music, and social habits, all of which are mimicry exercises that are transmitted by languages of sound, symbol, and motion.

> Given children's early competence in understanding others, why do they continue to fail classic ToM tasks for several years? ...It is not until children reach...around age 4, that they begin to use language to describe the connection between people's beliefs to their behaviors. (Geren 2009: 6,12)

CONVERSION DEVICES

PART FIVE

Intention

Mistaking Intentions

All four conversion devices—novelty, intention, recursion, and mirroring—work as much on a cognitive and seemingly automatic level as they do on a gross motor one. Meaning what we do as a matter of opinion or judgment, as opposed to what is hot-wired into our brains. It is impossible to ascertain where one mediating response, say 'intention,' yields to another such as 'recursion.'

For example, you can 'fake' throwing your dog a bone because he has some kind of internalized motion graphic by which he groups sequential behaviors together to indicate the intention of throwing, with some links or 'chunking' more prominent than others. He really has no choice but to generalize and formulate predictive patterns. He has no other means by which to operate, given his physical limitations. There is a certain way his eyes can see, a certain angle from which he sees the world, a certain energy and temperament by which he needs to be satisfied with desires and curiosities. We are no different.

And just like our animal brethren, we can't know all angles and attributes of our environment. I do not know how the underside of a Columbine flower looks at dawn because I am always taller than it. But we do decide the salience of some characterizations in context with others just as other animals do. This leaves just enough wiggle room for mistakes. For example, Motmot birds have an instinctive alarm for the poisonous coral snake, which has alternating red/yellow striping. Paint a stick with it and they go nuts. Paint a stick another way and they don't. Still, it's just a stick (Hauber 2010; Dugatkin 2010; Purves 2008).

In the same way, male guppies can be fooled into mounting female dummies just as Erasmus Darwin (Charles's grandfather) fooled his frogs into attacking glowing coals, which they mistook for fireflies. And on a personal and very non-scientific note, when I was first married and living in Mexico, evening would bring these enormous bulbous flies with tiny wings. We would sit and watch them crash into walls and fall to the floor, inevitably to summon forth whatever leftover juice they had and repeat their kamikaze tricks. There was something about the light on the wall that had the right kind of attributes arranged in precisely right way to suggest something else in their natural environment.

The question is where the 'intention' for their actions originated. Was it in the random associating of familiar environments or was it a preset desire that a particular activity must be happening at that moment?

But the natural environment also does the fooling – like the Australian Wasp Mimetic Tongue Orchid (yes, that's the name), which mimics the female wasp so effectively that the poor male fertilizes the flower (Hauber 2010). This belies the Darwinian notion of rigid genetic behavior and leaves enough doubt as to the adaptive nature of coding through cultural incentives, but within limits. For example, a female guppy can 'decide' to break with mating tradition and seek a drabber male, with the other 'girls' emulating her behavior but only across a few generations (Dugatkin 2010). Eventually, the coloration of the male guppy must not be too 'drab' or the survival coding will reject it as diseased.

That tiny bit of wiggle room sheds light on the fact that even among animals, genetics alone cannot account for the dynamic cognitization of visualizing. If this were so, animals like birds, snakes, and monkeys could not misread the intentional signals of their environment, despite our messing around with their culturalization.

Or as Marc Hauber noted:

> Perhaps the greatest puzzle of communication system theory is how to reconcile the apparent evolutionary stability of signal design and information content with the observed ontogenetic unpredictability and plasticity of signal production, perception and decoding. (Hauber 2010: 191)

Rhesus monkeys raised in a lab who had no fear of snakes were asked to 'watch' and therefore imitate the behavior of others raised in the wild to acquire a new 'search alarm' (Rizzollati 1996; Shipton 2009; Loizos 2006). That this coding lapsed after three months makes one wonder if a little Lamarckian theorizing about the inheritance of adaptive behavioral traits might have some merit. And chimps who share 99% of our genetic code do not perform all functions identically and therefore genetically. They demonstrate different 'styles' for nut-cracking depending on their habitat (Ings 2007; Tomasello 1994a; Turner 2008; Shipton 2009). And some unique personalities perform tricks that become cultural memes of variable duration.

Mimicry and emulation, when they have distinct, transitive merit attached, that is, distinct goal-oriented *chaîne opératoires* (Dugatkin 2010), propagate across time. In fact, the mirror system identified in the F5 area of the macaque monkey finds that activation of these cells is decidedly intentional.

When imitation behavior has no task reward, the mirror neurons do not fire.

Mirroring- again

Which brings us to the overlapping of novelty and intention with mirroring as a mediating device on which 'image-creation' is predicated. Returning to primates, Jane Goodall, Desmond Morris, and many more have found them to be constantly vigilant of their conspecific's behavior (Loizos 2006). It has been reported that they are so nervous about social outcomes, particularly at the discretion of their troop leader, that they attentively watch for facial changes to react. We do too. The difference is that they do not mentalize a sufficiently robust face caricature to anticipate responses, as even our very children do. Some anthropologists have a theory about this difference.

How distance seeds intention and imagery

Clive Gamble (Pryor 2003) ascribes the notion of physical proximity to a very 'shallow' social understanding, particularly when explaining the dearth of Paleolithic freestanding artifacts. Here's how. For non-human primates, the notion of novelty is highly circumscribed and short-lived, as it might have been for most hominids before the Sapiens branch swung into view. When proximity to one's group is close because the population is so small, as it is with the great apes, which includes chimps (Shipton 2010; Botha 2010; Loizos 2006; Turner 2008; Ings 2007; Pryor 2003), there is little motivation for exaggerating observations across time and space because everything is so temporal and immediate.

Purposeful memorizing is of little necessity. Primate relations are highly proximal, very responsive between two subjects, but not across absences or populations. They tend to be casual creatures, moving in and out of troops, and highly independent. Gamble suggests that the larger and more distal (i.e., spread out) the community such as early Cro-Magnons, the more need there was to anticipate behavior because the distances were physically vaster, both by virtue of troop size and the inevitable dilution of immediacy due to crowding.

Interesting.

Consider the proximal/distal adaptations you make in your own life. When your troop is limited to your 'toddler,' no one obstructs your vision so you can rely on moment to moment observations. Accessibility is a direct determinant of one's need to anticipate behavior. When you enroll him in kindergarten, you have less time to watch his face with gestures, so you extrapolate which expressions are portentous and which are benign. You no longer have the luxury of endless nuance and immediate vindication.

The larger the boundary of your community becomes, and the more populous, the more urgent the task for developing a lexicon of warning devices. When those devices can become transferable across time, space, and culture, they serve as memory caches. The impulse for image-creation, as precisely these freestanding prompts, in turn accelerates community mindedness, and of course, theory of mindedness.

Life Histories and Neural Motifs

It begins at birth. A normal baby of eight months has already learned to follow its parents' eyes, first to confirm they are being watched and connecting with the child's actions (Geren 2009; Giovennelli 2006; Shipton 2010; Baron Cohen 1999; Ings 2007; Iacobini 2003; Rizzollati 1996). They also track the mother's eyes as pointers in a new world and follow accordingly. These little dark dots are really shifting bullseye targets. At the center of a white field is the dark dot. Eyes are the first real imitation paradigms we learn for seeking our place, our relationship to space and our habits. Infants infer intention and novelty by means of visual signage, which occurs as an exchange of one stream of multisensory data for another.

We surely notice how swiftly these paired little dark spots jump around, and even learn about 'motion' from it. Babies do it as we all do it, and that is by means of the peripheral accompaniment of facial muscles, body gesture, vocalizations, and ambient effects. They are all within a child's visual field. To borrow the *Nike* branded term, eyes are indicators of 'swoosh.' Let me refer you to our friend, the tiny ant, for which communication works through a variety of signals (Holldobler 2010).

> A signal can be composed of many components, transmitted simultaneously or in tightly paced sequences...

This is also something Darwin brought forward in his book '*The Expressions of the Emotions in Man and Animals,*' published in 1872.

> ...the intensity of communication by language is much enhanced by the expressive movements of face and body.

Witness the impending 'time out!' coming down on your toddler by the scowl on your face and the widening of your eyes.

But the cues are even subtler and more instantaneous than that with an effect that directly impacts our immediate behavior. In 1875, Sigmund Exner (Purves 2008; Livingstone 2008, etc.) discerned that the human eye reads two brief stationary flashes as a single motion. Called the *phi* phenomenon, it's the trick we use in viewing movies by cognitively fusing separate frames of imagery. This is different than 'flicker,' which addresses our optical limitations when parsing the speed of the flashes.

What is really being 'figured out' is the 'notification' about intended motion. It's not so much what is conspicuous about intended movement because there are many things that start to rustle and change, or 'swoosh,' in advance of it. It's what we *decide* about how to read it.

How different is that from an infant's perception of motion by watching parental eyes saccade three times a second? A single glance, much like a snippet of film, constitutes a string of multiple fixations. What are the findings on a baby's linking ocular gyrations with the anticipation of body motion. How odd or even frightening would it be for them to predict motion and emotion from, say, the indication of a mother's eyes that is not followed by the anticipated effect? If she does not follow through with physical motion and word/sounds. It would be scary indeed.

The ability to conduct such experiments would also be difficult.

Although we can't yet walk, our neuroanatomy can prognosticate motor behavior from this signage, particularly by nine months when our hippocampus is fully operational and our long-term memory establishes firm attachments to caregivers.

> Simply put, the sensory stimuli that represent possible goals must be combined with cognitively derived signals that reflect the behavioral context in which they occur. (Wyder 2004)

A tall order, and much like an orchestra of sensory streams, highly in need of a talented conductor. Whether you ascribe that particular talent to the thalamus as many do, there is no way to conduct all the parts without the curious Konio neurons, which most likely contribute decisively to this 'context dependent linkage of sensory signals and saccadic commands' (Wyder 2004). Call it the 'feeling of knowing.'

This 'feeling of knowing' as already noted, is the sensation of sliding a puzzle piece into that phantom slot, of slipping sensory inputs into preexisting imitations. I know I promised to try to avoid this kind of talk. But I want you to understand that the imitative paradigms to which I refer are not initially symbolic. They are not crafted by means of taught stories and equations. In fact, they seem to be unconscious.

The Feeling of Knowing...

...is constructed of multiple sensations. It is never 'flat' because the sensory stream is not singular. Frankly, when is it ever? Just as a voxel describes the cubic byte of one millimeter of brain, 'the feeling of knowing' is an intra-dependent cubic sensation. Enter the curious Koniocellular cells, which are the somatosensory integration neurons of the thalamic lateral geniculate nucleus (Purves 2008; Allman 2011). Lodged between the distinct six layers of Magno and Parvo cells, they intra-layer themselves like brick-pointing mortar and are vital to holding up the complex edifice of cognition. If the konios integrate multiple sensations, they are as far as this author is concerned the essential 'synthesizers' of visualization. And visualization is highly cubic.

***

Let's go back to the interpretation of these ridiculously small eye dots, which become more descriptive as we get older because the implications of their movements have been autobiographically seared into our neural connections. As a practitioner of fine arts, I can say that the placement of these spots, as specific as the tiny pupillary points with or without (usually without) a cornea, is the magnetic target we manipulate for mood-enhancing advantage. Those who dismiss these minutiae strip the image of immediacy and power. Yet in an overall, waist-up portrait, they constitute far less than one-millionth of the space.

How can such miniscule marks command such attention? Worse even, how can our cognition become so tuned to the behavioral and emotive ramifications of the seeming infinitely minute mapping of these points within the lidded boundary of the eye shape? We don't need (Alfred) Yarbus lines (Matlin 2004; Purves 2008; Ings 2008) to tell us, just watch a baby.

VENs and the Merging of Motion with Shape

Konios need VENs. In 2005, John Allman et al (2010) suggested that the Von Economo Neurons (already discovered in the late 19th century but forgotten), located in the inferior (ventral) anterior insulae, an area previously identified with decision-making and some physiological changes, were triggered for negative feedback in eye reflection.

What does this mean? Well, that we have 'rapid intuition circuitry,' '...which like perceptual awareness involves immediate effortless awareness' (Allman 2010:5-21). Except no awareness is really *ex-nihilo* effortless, though it might become so over time with the testing of multiple sensory contexts.

An 'aha!' moment is a rapid recognition event, emphasis on 're-cognitize', not an inborn reflex. Or is it? It occurs, for example, when you gaze into another's eyes whose pupil behavior is discordant from your own. This lack of re-projected imitation or mirroring sends an alert of discordance and activates the anterior insular and anterior cingulate cortices among other key clusters.

We already discussed this discordant reaction in typical people. The problem is, how do we 'know' that the constrained eye movement or dilation is an indicator of mood and movement in someone else if we have not observed ourselves constantly in a mirror? I suppose one could ask the same of an angry old buck fighting a younger one to maintain his prominence. Why not fight an upstart goat? In fact, how do all animals know to identify with friend or foe of their own species?

This is similar to the sympathetic movements that Darwin enjoyed recounting, where men move their feet when they see a performer 'make his spring (leap)' (Darwin 2009:7). Or wincing when someone is suddenly put in an awkward position, especially someone close to us. If it is based on identification, the obvious question is how does that get set up to begin with?

A possible answer might be that this kind of reflection is redundant if there are automatic neural mechanisms for fabricating internal copies '...of an observed action that is largely indistinguishable from an action performed by the self...' (Iacobini 2003:1123-1128). The key concept being biological action or movement. For it is observed biological behavior that matters a whole lot such that there is a neural mapping of an observed biological action that reverberates commonality by linking the actor with the observer. It's some kind of abstract mapping that correlates with the abstract mapping we internalize for our own physicality.

However, assuming one's own typicality, as already mentioned, for children's emergent Theory of Mind around age five does not mean that the internal patterning for it is coeval. Hardly. And since it involves visualization, could this obvious motion and shape behavior activate all of our visual cortex, both the ventral (i.e., shape) and dorsal (i.e. motion) streams?

Point light motion

We all encounter vernacular point light figures when navigate city streets. More minimalist is the 11 to 13 point light human body motion paradigms for which much research work has been undertaken (Hunt

2008; Courtine 2003; Vaina 2001, etc). How do we seem to know much better that these dots or points of light are human beings when they are in motion rather than static? Or that patients with impairment in their visual motion pathways '...can reliably recognize human actions in point light displays?' (Vaina 2001: 301–307). One would think this impossible for them. No, something else is going on or we have underestimated the differentiations of the primary visual pathways. While a number of cortical areas have been identified as active for this perception such as the superior temporal sulcus and poly-sensory area, I have to call your attention to how we cross city streets all over the world:

Most major cities have pedestrian crossing signs. These tend to be a form of point light images or just light shapes. They suggest a body in motion...your body in motion. They are technically static because the dots or the shape don't change within the image. However, they are motile by way of the effect from the book-ended flashes of the 'stop sign' motifs that ask us to stay put.

Sigmund Exner, as early as 1868 while writing his doctoral thesis in Heidelberg under Herman Von Helmholtz, began realizing that their appeared to be an impression of motion in the peripheral field of vision based on very little suggestion. Later, in a variety of tracts and eventually a book 'On Seeing Movement' published in 1876, he pointed out that two independent flashes are interpreted as a single motion. Or that the addition or subtraction of objects within the field of vision gives the same impression of activity. He suggested that a group of bright spots on a dark surface get pushed to the periphery of the field of vision and are not notable for their number. Clearly, he had discovered the behavior of rods.

But the kicker was that:

> ...as soon as one such spot is added to the existing ones or one disappears from the group an active impression occurs—one might be inclined to say that 'something moved' within their field of vision. (Shuler 2016:92)

We interpret the flashing of changing signs as motion, and it is not necessarily in our peripheral field of vision. Fascinating about these point light renderings is their variation within a general scheme. Rarely are there as few as eleven points used, though sometimes lines replace dots. But in all cases, we get the gist from these simple marks: *Hurry up and walk fast*. It is an effective imitation of movement, mediated by an interpretation of intention from a set of organized dots or shapes.

The point lights are a bit different. Nothing is subtracted, bracketed, or removed. Instead, it is a description of motion from shapes with the implied and subtle advert of 'speed.' Do we 'get it' because we project an imitation of our active selves on the world about walking just as we eventually understand how to read a hostile response from someone's gaze because we are already familiar with it in ourselves?

VENs Again: Underestimate them at your peril

The location of VENs, sometimes called the 'sentient self' cells, are found in a small variety of places. Among them, the anterior cingulate cortex and frontal insulae. This is curious. Sometimes referred to as a lobe in its own right, the insulae lie deep behind another cortical covering, the operculari, which means 'covering'. The proximity of these two clusters is essential for self-perception through our propioceptive (literally, self-awareness) sensations such as touch, feel, balance, and limb movement, in addition to emotional processing and social awareness.

The curious and counterintuitive part of this is that autists do not have fewer of these bipolar cells in their Fronto Insular cortex, but an increase in ratio to their pyramidal cells in their layer five. The visual description alone of these unique cells is meaningful. They are sparse in dendrites and vertically symmetrical in their axons out from a central spindle shaped soma, or the hub of the cell. Hence, they are often referred to as spindle cells.

However, VENs for autists seem to have enlarged somas and longer corkscrewed dendrites. On the surface, this appears to be a far more hardworking cell if not an overworked cell. Factor in its role for determining differences or 'disambiguating,' which is an overblown word that just means clarifying something, and we get a sense of the imitation factor embedded in the processing. The reason is that you can't clarify something unless you know what it is not and how it fails to match up with a preexisting idea.

What constricts autists from fluid and typical operations might in part be their over identification, or at least their attempts to over-identify with others, that they are hyper-allocentric, not egocentric. This then follows with supportive expressions from high-performing autists who explain the need to constantly gather up their escaping body parts into a central whole. It is a constant challenge that results in what the normal world sees as manic obsessive centripetal actions like spinning, flapping arms and repetitions.

Some point to this fronto interior insulae area of the brain for the formation of a paradigm for selfness, a mapping out of one's sensory extensions as an independent object. This is something we shall revisit in our conclusion about synesthesia and art. Far more interesting is that these VENs are rare at birth and increase in number through the first eight months, much like our retinal cones. At birth, we only 'see' with our luminance sensitive rods in our retinal peripheries. Just as an aside, rods have more pigment (i.e., rhodopsin) than cones, and can detect lower light. Babies are therefore 50 times more sensitive to light and have scotopic vision, or low-light vision. Cats have eight times more rods and ten times fewer cones than we do, which explains why they are crepuscular hunters, favoring dawn and twilight. Now, back to VENs.

VENs tend to populate asymmetrically in the right side which is also the larger hemisphere. To what end? Well, also interesting is that just like the *de facto* increased rate of cell birth in the hippocampus for food-hoarding birds like jays and chickadees, which must remember and retrieve from thousands of caches in comparison to those that do not, a child must build up 'relationship caches' for memory of all facial angles of life-sustaining associates—trusted versus untrusted caregivers.

These are interior maps or imitation devices both of oneself and others that also populate over time and eventually become centralized in a part of the visual cortex called the fusiform face area. Generally, this recognition hub in the ventral stream of the temporal lobe of the fusiform gyrus is also considerably larger on the right side, sometimes almost twice as large. I have always wondered how the seeding of these object hubs in the extrastriate cortex of our visual system comparatively develop for the blind who must construct facial paradigms by tactile and audial prompts, or visualizations that are not optically derived (Ostrovsky 2006).

Automatic Mirroring

As already suggested, 'mirroring' is a neural substrate for imitation too. Outwardly, we see this '...when imitating, human infants either selectively reproduce the intentional, but not the accidental of adults' (Shipton 2010: 197).

How on earth do they know? At this point, our mirror neurons, or rather neurons in our (ventral Brodmann 6) premotor cortex and the caudal sector of the anterior frontal gyrus, become activated. The latter area, also known as the pars opercularis mentioned above, is one of three parts of Broca's Area for language production (also known as Brodmann's 44), and fires with an internal stimulation for intentional behavior, 'indicating that the default function of these neurons is to interpret actions as intentional and codes not just the goal of the action but the way it is delivered' (Binkofski 2000). There's the clue --- interesting.

Therefore, 'intention,' conservatively speaking, is highly stimulative for converting sensory inputs into copying responses. It's as if our cortex needs to first set up a premotor reciprocity system for representation or an imitative framework that will serve us later as we build in other motor signals as in pictures and eventually language.

Clearly, 'imitation' is a concept that has life-sustaining force. It is something we understand very early on, be it copying a smile and the benign cues it signals onward to procedural mimicry, including walking. It seems logical and certainly anecdotally suggestive that these mirroring routines are neurally set up or prefigured before being reproduced. I suggest that it is as if our visualization cognition is partially in place, perhaps audial too, necessarily prefiguring an imitative design for which the kinesthetic sensations become fully integrated and matched when the time comes.

In other words, we already have some kind of a roadmap for walking before we do it. And for complex speech, long before we utter a word. Very young children know many words and syntax before they speak. Just as I alluded to regarding a five-year-old's 'Theory of Mind,' the motif must be long there on a neural basis. Though I agree with many like Jesse Snedeker, Elizabeth Spelke, and others who tend to set age four as the ToM threshold, perhaps much earlier. The physical behavior of vocalization follows in due course.

The Feeling of Seeing

When we read or listen to familiar music, we truly hear ourselves inwardly saying the words. We mouth them as we imagine sounds emanating forth. Our palate muscles flex. Cheek muscles too. For tunes, songs, music, our shoulders lift. We sway, sometimes visibly but more often just engage in some way the swaying muscles. Our heads tilt, necks crane, torsos contract. We move. Our mini-self silently speaks, though we are incredibly close to aurally hearing the imagined sounds. When we observe a foot, especially when drawing, but certainly when we imagine one, we 'feel it' either because the appropriate muscles slightly tighten or we direct our focus immediately to the explicit sensations of our 'foot.'

All artists know this to such an extent that first lessons in life drawing begin with 'walk around the model and feel her dimension in space, the thrust of the body, etc.' Translation: *Be* that body yourself. During 'Simon Says,' our non-language, copying reflex triggers our premotor cortex before action is undertaken. Just as Benjamin Libet and Edwin H. Land pointed out, we perform in the past tense, where our actions live in a time lapse. In other words, you cannot perform unless you have already executed the action in your brain.

There is a whole world of study devoted to human reaction times called mental chronometry, the lapses between the introduction of a stimulus and our counteraction or response. But the brain is working all along and automatically configuring the potential for action whether we undertake it or not. Deep within, there develops outwardly a 'threshold level of awareness of a sensation,' a term Libet uses. Who and what decides which of the many potentials gets activation? How is the intention for this derived? Libet studied the involuntary time lapses of readiness potentials before a voluntary action or decision to override them. At an average of about one second or 800ms to 550ms '...cerebral initiation of a spontaneous voluntary act begins unconsciously' (Libet 1985), with electrophysiological responses recorded on the scalp.

Possible awareness of a decision looming occurs at around 300ms. Still, it allows for a solid 150ms before an action response to be considered fully, to be intended or thwarted. As Libet says, we still have time to 'veto' it. Well, not just 'it,' but many many possible permutations. Why a certain few rise to the surface is a wonderful and awesome question that continues to perplex and goad us. But let's not get too far afield of this discussion's premise regarding imitation.

It has also been found that action words alone can tense us. Part of that tension derives from suppressing the activation of a mimetic response. Reading or hearing them triggers the same readiness potentials discussed above, and thus there is a visual component derived from graphics (e.g., reading letters) too that initiates mimicry. Children love Simon Says because they are experts and are still very much tuned to consciously doing by seeing others doing before performing and certainly before speaking.

> The creation of an internal copy of an observed action that is largely indistinguishable from an action performed by the self, places the observer in the perspective of the actor. (Heiser 2003:1123)

In one respect (among others), it's as if imitation teaches us sensory procedure rather than the reverse. Therefore, action goals have a beginning, middle, and end, and in turn format our brains for syntax, the prioritizing of salient associations. But there is a more momentous driver and organizer for syntax with the realization that 'I am that.' This is the identification of 'self' as a non-unique but rather typical and highly conforming object that is inevitably linked or mirrored with a host of ineffably shared behaviors and qualities contained by like objects.

It's a cognitive application just like a computer one where the format necessarily organizes incoming data. This overlapping of our visualization responsiveness with our motor response might render us the uber-imitative breeder reactor of all species. But then again, that could be assuming that others don't parse their world with as copious mirroring instincts as we do.

One reason many can get away with saying this has to do with the kind and amount of garbage we leave. Our creative trash clutters the planet and outlives every generation, epoch, and evolutionary twist and turn. In graves, in pits, on stone, in caves, in mounds, under earth, in heaps, in cached websites, and well, it really doesn't matter how effective any of this is, how clumsy the fabrications of our world, or how off-base they can seem. All that matters is the time and brain cells invested in purloining in some way what we encounter outside our bodies, formatted through the sensibilities and limitations of those bodies as freestanding objects.

Mirrors

'Mirroring' neurons redound to the inevitability of our impulse for imitative imaging. Consequently, we just can't help our so-called creative impulses. They begin as deeply neural, mirroring reflexes and flower forth. Not everyone smiles back when you do, but if they don't, it's because they have suppressed the underlying impulse to repeat what a similar likeness is doing. This kind of decision is so swift but so decisive.

Most important is that it teases the inevitability of some kind of hardwired 'decider' that has expectations of outcomes based on equally hardwired presumptions. In fact, that it purposefully seeks certain outcomes. Those expectations are based on matching one's own physical appearance with some 'other' one. We assume these neurons exist based on consistent recorded activities in certain locations like the frontal and inferior parietal cortex rather than in the identification of a specific kind of mirroring cell. The search for them continues, though.

'Mirroring' cannot be done without merging the knowledge of one's own body motion with an exterior visual match. For example, monkeys cannot perform the mirror mark test or MSR (mirror self-recognition), where the forehead (usually) is marked and they are asked or observed for pointing to it on themselves. Apes can do this better because they have an inordinate fascination with their own bodies and the visual anomalies they constantly seek. Grooming is an example of this. What's important is that embedded in mirroring behavior and therefore mimicry is a distinct decision to 'seek and ye shall find.'

That these curious cells are still putative, matters less than the fascinating activation of neural clusters for tasks that previously were expected to bypass them. FMRI readings bear out activation of the posterior sector of Broca's Area in the posterior frontal lobe (i.e., inferior frontal gyrus) right around the enormous geographical divide of the Sylvian Fissure. Why do they also 'light' up during this behavior?

Furled

If not for this deep sulcus or rift, our brains unfolded would seem better suited to fit inside the cranium of a pterodactyl. This fissure is the fold resulting from our cortex flipped back on itself, so that the particular region in question, also identified as Brodmann 44, lies caudal (in the rear of) our premotor strip, and both are therefore conveniently tucked nicely near the all-important thalamus and optic chiasm. Unfolded, this wouldn't be the case. If one were told that this Brodmann 44 region is specific for speech comprehension and syntax, it might be unsurprising to also discover how it reverberates back and forth with motor sensations and sensory planning.

Take unfurled DNA - a strand of which measures about ten feet. But that's not how it exists in nature. It is so tightly coiled that it fits inside the nucleus of a cell, altering the distances between segments so vastly that parts unfurled and distant from another now become snug bedfellows. In other words, the normal, three-dimensional function of genetic relationships makes proximal and interacting what is technically analyzed as linear and distantly apart.

Or better still, just stop for a moment and look at your hand. Spread your fingers wide. Notice how far apart the ring finger is from the thumb. There's a pen to pick up on the table. Pick it up. Can't do it? That's because spread wide as individual units, they are utterly dysfunctional. Sure, we know it as the opposable thumb, but you could see the same thing happening without using it. Function fosters this integration. Contiguity supports influence and speed regardless of what the absolute forms unto themselves suggest.

Taken a step further. The part of Broca's Area in question, also known as the Pars Opercularis, previously mentioned, mirrors words that have task-oriented or intentional ramifications involving action words referring to face, arm, leg, and fingers (Heiser 2003; Binkofski 2000; Wyder 2004; Osaka 2008; Vaina 2001). And in passive-reading tests, areas in the adjacent premotor strip are also activated.

> These results demonstrate that the reading of words referring to actions performed with different body parts activates the motor and premotor cortex in a somatotopic fashion. (Hauk 2004)

What all this seems to say is that we rehearse before we do. Another way to put this is that our actions imitate a neural copy. But even more illuminating is that this area belies the hard and fast belief that language precedes image-creation. (Leakey 1993; Livingstone 2008; White 1992, etc)

More than word comprehension, observing actions that have an egocentric fulcrum to them such as imagining oneself as the observer of one's own actions or imagining your finger drawing an endless circle have an accelerated responsiveness in this area. For example, Ferdinand Binkofski asked his subjects to observe themselves moving their right index fingers following a target with eyes shut tight. I dare say, a complex thought experiment.

> During imagery of one's own limb motion from observer's perspective there was left hemisphere activation of 44 versus imagery of spatial target motion in the right hemishphere 44. (Binkofski et al. 2000:280)

Left side favors self-oriented imagery; right favors abstract?

Children learn to visualize by physically testing the environment by touch, extension, and mobility. When we draw a line, it is based on linear body movement most delightedly confirmed in the young when they see their own tracks in the sand or snow. There is something very curious going on here. Is their Pars Operculari lighting up? Is an interior graphic that imitates their behavior as an object under construction?

Synesthesia

> _...Or what Sir Francis Galton first described as the_
> _'peculiar habit of mind.'_

In the human sensory motor system, the exchange or conversion of one modal input for another is called 'capture.' This is, for example, the immediate translation of a touch sensation into a visual one, or a sound sensation into a kinesthetic, or haptic sensation or graphic symbol for a sound effect. Image-creation is helpless without this.

Better still, 'synesthesia,' or 'perceiving together,' is a powerful stimulus for imitation that I suggest drives the impulse to craft plastic imitations *even before* the conscious need to heighten search and seeking perception.

*

Our genetic forefathers, the great Middle Miocene apes of Africa, couldn't have evolved if they weren't synesthesiacs with a keen ability to translate the sensation for gravity, of motion, and falling by visualizing distance and volume when swinging through the arboreal canopy of their rainforest habitat (Turner 2008). Cognitive assumptions had to be made, tested, and confirmed over time that became the operative matrix of their sensory motor behavior.

Many would not call this synesthesia because there is a cause-and-effect sequence. The problem is that it is extremely difficult to determine this when the rapidity of the cause becoming an effect is so efficiently internalized that it becomes essentially immediate. It becomes a balanced equation. But don't discount fear and emotion which are just as valid trigger sensations for our magnificently synesthesiac minds such that the horror of simian slippage persists in us even to this day. And just as an aside, we are still inevitably drawn to the arboreal heights.

We use them for scouting and ceremonial acts. Or just for challenges. Take the Citibank rock-climbing commercial, with the young woman seeking the highest butte as the real 'rock she covets instead of a diamond.' Or the fact that men like to propose on the observation deck of tall buildings or that pilgrimages coil up mountains to shrines perched at dizzying altitudes. Saint Francis of Assisi, as with many, sought vertiginous heights for his reclusive and numinous inspiration. We covet the eagle-eye perspective when and where we can, climbing as high as we can go, but we don't want to fall.

We love to be scared. We also love the Eiffel Tower.

Avoiding the shock of slippage, no doubt, worked in tandem with the evolving sensitivity of touch in great apes and our own fingertips with the mental projection of the sturdiness of branches for bearing their weight and momentum. The triggered scenarios, though incredibly fast-moving, are imitative scenarios too; they combine visualization with haptics and the sensation of thrust and weight resistance in the neuro-sensors of joints called spindles. These cascading or rushing mental scenarios 'imitate' their three-dimensional environment. They become paradigms on which minute decisions are made. But none of these ideations could coalesce into vital judgments without emotion acting as cognitive glue, etching deep synaptic recovery routes for long-term memory.

Mechanoreceptors

'Imitation' through this kind of projection off such seemingly inconsequential anatomy as fingertips and palms is a case in point. We discussed this in Chapter 2, but it needs repeating. For many of us, we come to 'see' with them. There are at least four layers of mechanoreceptors lodged in the epidermis of our fingers that vary by density from finger to finger, and distinguish the individual talents of, say, the index finger from the third finger based on the kind of cell that predominates. I mention this only to drive home the speciation of our sensory inputting to the neural cortex.

Merkel cells located in the epidermal sweat ridges or fingerprints, for example, are 'slow adapting' sensors that affer or send inputs gradually back to the somatosensory cortex. These cells have the highest spatial resolution (as determined by the two points of a caliper) and can distinguish details of 0.5 millimeters, as opposed to the resolution sensitivity of, say, your forearm epidermis, which is much sloppier and can determine objectivity that is spaced only 40 millimeters apart. No wonder then that these sensors in our fingers discern points and edges, and more importantly, curvature, which makes them so suitable to apes for assessing the weight-bearing capability of branches fast enough to avert a disaster.

There are three other known 'propioceptors' (receptors for self) in our fingertips, each tasked differently based on which kind of receptor and clumsy at discerning fine variation. Texture, however, it's awfully good at, though I cannot enumerate or isolate small sensations like bumps. But my index finger can. The reason is that the mechanoreceptor in the tip of my middle finger is the rapid firing 'Meissner' afferent (located in the dermal papillae, lying closest to the skin's surface, and constituting over 40% of the innervation for the hand) that shuts down with redundancy.

Texture is redundant; no need to send back endless messages about the exact number of individual hairs on my cat's neck. My brain is not set up to count it—too much noise and distraction. No wonder then that my index finger is my pointer finger, and that which I instinctively activate when determining the contour of an object that I see, or the direction of something important. I simply can't help using it. The pencil I use tracks my finger, trying to grab at a contour across space. Every tiny child knows this by pointing toward an object and watching his mother's eyes to ensure she is following.

It's our smart antenna finger for a reason. I suggest you try isolating the contour of a face from its environmental context. You will note the immediate sensation of your 'smart' index finger pulling forward and wanting to point or 'carve it out.' If you are especially 'aware,' you will also feel a sensation of pressure and cupping in your palm, but not to the same extent as you would were you to gaze attentively at a tree branch.

When visualized, there are just some things our species has been more hardwired to touch than others. This too is the interpolation of sensory inputs and activations typical for synesthesia. My index finger 'sees.' Eventually, my hand alone might determine what an object is, what we call stereognosis. Only atypicals lack this (i.e. astereognosis). Though I feel a very strong impulse to open my eyes and check, don't you? The number of times in a given day we react synesthetically is of mind-boggling frequency. But all of this sensory conversion interplay is just another way to explain the imitative changeup between our senses as we evaluate one sensation in terms of another.

On a City Bus

The first time all this hit me was when I was nine years old and sitting on a city bus. Settling in directly opposite, I watched in wonder as a gentleman emphatically clutched the metal pole by draping his palm around it as his fingers would follow and wrap around it. The entire gesture of his elbow, the tilt of his shoulders, and thrust of his body indicated a strong belief that his 'fingers' were 'leading' the entire grasping movement and enjoying the feel of the metal. Except he had no fingers. His delight in using 'them' and his desire to 'relive' the gesture by wrapping and re-wrapping his phantom fingers around the pole indicated some residual feelings, however odd it might have looked. And here's the kicker. The entire caricaturized expression of his body in motion made *me* 'feel' those fingers he had lost. I couldn't help but repeat in my head the feel and action of those missing fingers with the added dimension of also 'feeling' his fingerless palm as my own palm. Pretty convoluted a visual response on my part. But it was the inevitability of mirroring him that fascinated. I was essentially his victim. We all are. There is really no escaping just this kind of thing in large and small measure throughout the day and life. I wasn't mirroring his actions; I was mirroring his cognition and then mirroring his sensations. I understood his intent. Then I felt it.

Brooklyn and Cambridge 2011-2015, edited 2016-2017

Alexandra Kraeler Corbin

Bibliography:

Allman, John et al (2010) 'The Von Economo neurons in Fronto insular and anterior cingulate cortex in great apes and man', *Brain Structure Function,* 214:495-517

Allman, John et al (2005) 'Intuition and Autism: A possible role for Von Economo Neurons', *Trends in Cognitive Science* v. 9, i. 8:367-373

Arnheim, R. (1990) 'Perceptual aspects of art for the blind', *Journal of Aesthetic Education,* 24:57-65

Arnold, Derek et al (2007) 'Staying focused: A functional account of perceptual suppression during binocular rivalry' *Journal of Vision,* v. 7:7, Article 7

Arnold, Derek (2008) *'Perceived Size and Spatial Coding'* The Journal of Neuroscience, 4 June 2008, 28(23):5954-5958

Averbach, E. and Coriell, A. S. (1961) 'Short-Term Memory in Vision.' *Bell System Technical Journal,* 40: 309-328

Averbach, E. and Sperling, G. (1961) 'Short term storage of information in Vision', in *Information Theory,* ed. by Cherry. C., (Butterworth and Co., Wash. DC) pp. 196-211

Arnold, Mathias (2004) *Henri de Toulouse Lautrec: The Theatre of Life,* (Taschen, Paris)

Baddeley, Alan (2000) 'Short term memory and working memory', Chapter 5 in *'The Oxford Handbook of Memory',* ed. by Endel Tulving and Fergus Craik, (Oxford Univ. Press)

Bainbridge, David, (2008) *Beyond the Zonules of Zinn,* (Harvard University Press, Cambridge)

Ball, Philip (2001) *Bright Earth,* Farrar, (Straus, Giroux, New York)

Baron-Cohen, Simon et al (2001) 'Theory of Mind in Normal Development and Autism' *Prisme,* 34:174-183

Baron-Cohen, Simon (1995) *'Mind Blindness: An essay on Autism and Theory of Mind,* (MIT Press, MA)

Baron-Cohen, Simon, Johnson et al (2013) 'Is synesthesia more common in autism?' *Molecular Autism,* Nov. 20th

Barret, H. Clark et al (2007) 'The hominid entry into the cognitive niche' chapter 25 in *The Evolution of Mind,* ed. By Gangsted and Simpson, (Guilford Press, New York)

Battaglia, Peter et al (2003) 'Bayesian integration of visual and auditory signals for spatial localization', *Journal of Optical Society of America,* v. 20: no.7:1391-8

Bednarik, R (1995) 'Concept Mediated marking in the Lower Paleolithic', *Current Anthropology,* 36:4:605-34

Berti, Anna and Frassinnetti, Francesca (2000) 'When Far Becomes Near: Remapping of Space by Tool Use' *Journal of Cognitive Science* v. 12, no. 3:415-420

Bickerton, Derek (1995) *Language and Human Behavior,* (Univ. of Washington Press)

Bickerton, Derek (1990) *Language and Species* (University of Chicago Press)

Bicknell, Peter. J. (1969) 'Democritus' Theory of Pre-cognition', <u>Revue des Études Grecques</u> v. 82 no. 391

Binkofski et al (2000) 'Broca's region subserves imagery of motion: A combined cytoarchitectonic and fMRI study' in *Human Brain Mapping* v. 11:4

Binkofsky, Ferdinand and Buccino, Giovanni (2004) 'Motor functions for the Broca's Region' in *Brain and Language* 84:362-369

Blaut, J. M. (1987) 'Notes Towards a Theory of Mapping Behavior', *Children's Environments Quarterly,* 4:27-34

Blaut, J.M. (1991) 'Natural Mapping', *Transactions of the Institute of British Geographers,* (The Royal Geographical Society, London) 16:2 pp. 55-74

Blaut, J., Stea, D. et al (2003) 'Mapping as a Cultural and Cognitive Universal' *Annals of the Association of American Geographers',* 93:1

Blazhenkova, Olesya and Kozhevnikov, Maria (2010) 'Visual-object ability: A new dimension of non-verbal intelligence,' *Cognition* 117(3):276-301

Botha, Rudolph (2010) 'On the Soundness of Inferring Modern Language from Symbolic Behavior', *Cambridge Archaeological Journal,* 20:3 pp. 345-56

Botha, R and Knight, Chris editors (2009) *The Prehistory of Language,* (Oxford University Press, UK)

Botvinick, Mathew M. et al (2004) 'Conflict monitoring and anterior cingulate cortex: an update', *Trends in Cognitive Science,* v. 8 no.12:539

Botha, R. and Knight, and Adams (1989) *Journal of Archaeological Method and Theory* September 2015, v. 22, i 3, pp. 952–979

Bril, Blandine et al (Jan. 2012) 'Functional Mastery of percussive technology in nut cracking and stone flaking actions...' *Philosophical Transactions of Royal Society,* v. 367, pp. 59-74

Brooks, Jessica and Cullen, Kathleen (2013) 'The Primate cerebellum selectively Encodes Unexpected Self Motion', *Current Biology:* v. 23 i. 11 pp. 947-955

Burkert, Walter (1974) 'Air -Imprints or Eidola: Democritus' Aetiology of Vision', Paper presented at *International Colloquium on Ancient Philosophy at Toledo*

Bush, George et al (June 2000) 'Cognitive and emotional influences in anterior cingulate cortex', *Trends in Cognitive Sciences* v.14:6

Buzsáki, György (2002) 'Theta Oscillation in the Hippocampus' *Neuron,* v. 33 i. 3:325-340

Bruce, Vicki and Young, Andy (1986) 'Understanding face recognition', *British Journal of Psychology,* 77:305-327

Caçola, Priscilla et al (2014) 'An age-related view of the role of object and spatial cognitive styles in distance estimating' *Journal of Cognitive Psychology* v. 26, no. 2:146-157

Caplovitz, Gideon et al (2008) 'Failures to see: Attentive Blank Stares revealed by change blindness', *Consciousness and Cognition* v. 17:877-886

Cardinali, Lucilla et al (2012) 'Grab and object with a tool and change your body: Tool use dependent changes of body representation for action' in. *Exp Brain Res* 218

Carter, Cameron S. et al (1998) 'The anterior cingulate cortex, error detection and the online monitoring of performance,' *Science,* v. 280:747

Cavanagh, Patrick (2005) 'The artist as neuroscientist' in *Nature:* v. 434:301-307

Cavanagh, Patrick et al, (2001) 'Attention based visual routines: Sprites', *Cognition* 80:47-60

Cavanagh, Patrick, Wang, Dina and Chao, Jessic 'Reflections in Art,' (Harvard Univ.)

Chao, Linda et al (1999) 'Attribute-based neural substrates in temporal cortex for perceiving and knowing about objects' in *Nature Neuroscience* 2:913-919

Clayton, Nicola et al (2007) 'Social cognition by food-caching corvids. The western scrub- jay as a natural psychologist' *Philosophical Transactions B of the Royal Society*

Corballis, (2010) 'Did Language evolve before speech?' from *The Evolution of Human Language* edited by Richard Larson et al, (Cambridge University, UK)

Courtine, Gregoire and Schieppati, M. (2003) 'Human walking along a curved path...etc.' *European Journal of Neuroscience,* 18:177-190

Critchley, Hugo D. (2004) 'Neural systems supporting interoceptive awareness', *Nature Neuroscience* v. 7 no. 2

Curtis, Rick (on line article on animal tracking) 12 pages www.ussartf.org/animal tracking

Darwin, Charles (1872) *'The expression of the emotions in man and animals'* published by John Murray, London

Dawkins, Richard (1976) *The Selfish Gene,* (Oxford University Press, UK) See chapter 11,'Memes: The New Replicators,'

Delagnes, Anne and Roche, Helen (2005) 'Late Pliocene hominid knapping skills: The case of Lokalalei 2C, West Turkana, Kenya', *Journal of Human Evolution,* v. 48 l:5:435-472

Doidge, Norman, (2007) *The Brain that Changes Itself,* (Penguin Books, New York)

Donald, Merlin, (2010) 'The Exographic Revolution: Neuropsychological Sequelae' in Malafouris L. & Renfrew, Colin, (eds.) *The Cognitive Life of Things: Recasting the boundaries of the mind.* (Cambridge, UK: McDonald Institute Monographs) pp. 71-79

Dugatkin, Alan, (2010) *The Imitation Factor; Evolution Beyond the Gene,* (The Free Press, New York)

Eichenbaum, Michael, (2014) 'Time cells in the hippocampus; a new dimension for mapping memories', *The National review of Neuroscience,* Nov.15(11):732-44

Evrard, Henry et al (2012) 'Von Economo neurons in the anterior Insula of the Macaque Monkey,' *Neuron 74,* 482-489

Faulstich, Paul, (2009) 'Comments: Notes on Memetics', *Rock Art Research,* 26:1

Fernando-Armesto, Felipe (2015) *A foot in the river,* Oxford University Press

Friston, Karl (2010) 'The free-energy principle: A unified brain theory?' *Nature Reviews/Neuroscience,* January 2010, online

Fragaszy, Dorothy (1998) 'How non-human primates use their hands' chapter 6 in *The Psychobiology of the Hand*, ed, by Kevin Connolly (Mackeith Publishing, London)

Germine, Laura T., Duchaine, Bradley and Nakayama, Ken (2010) 'Where cognitive development and aging meet: Face learning ability peaks after age 30', *Cognition,*118.002:201-210

Gilbert, Richard and Weisel, Torsten (1989) 'Columnar specificity of intrinsic horizontal and corticocortical connections in the cat visual cortex,' *Journal of Neuroscience* 9(7)

Giovannelli, Joyce Lynne, (2006), *Face Processing Abilities in Children with Autism,* PH. D Thesis, University of Pittsburgh

Goldenberg, Georg (2002) 'Loss of visual imagery: Neuropsychological evidence in search for a theory' in 'Commentary/Pylyshyn: Mental Imagery in Search of a Theory', *Behavioral and Brain Sciences 25:2*

Goldenberg, G and Spatt, J. (2009) 'Neural basis of tool use', *Brain* v. 132 i. 6

Grandin, Temple (2013) *The Autistic Brain: Thinking across the spectrum*, (Houghton Mifflin Harcourt)

Graves, Austin R. et al (2012) 'Hippocampal Pyramidal Neurons Comprise two distinct cell types that are counter-modulated by metabotropic receptors' in *Neuron,* v. 76:776-789

Green, Marc, 'Night Vision' in *Visual Expert Human Factors* on line page

Griffin, I. C., & Nobre, A.C. (2003) 'Orienting attention to locations in internal representations'. *Journal of Cognitive Neuroscience* 15:1176-1194.

Gsell, Paul, (1971) 'Mystery in Art', *Rodin on Art*, (Horizon, New York) 1971 (171-181)

Haidle, Miriam N. (2010), 'Working Memory Capacity and the Evolution of modern cognitive potential: Implications from animal and early human tool use', *Current Anthropology*, 51:S1:149-166)

Hardy, Arthur C. (1920) 'A study of the persistence of vision', *Psychology* of *PNAS* v. 6 p. 221

Hauber, Mark E. and Zuk, Marlene (2010), 'Social Influences on communication signals: From Honesty to exploitation' (chapter 8), in *Social Behavior: Genes, Ecology and Evolution*, ed. by Szekely, Tomas et al (Cambridge University Press, UK)

Hauk, Olaf, Johnsrude, I and Pulvermuller, F. (2004) 'Somatotopic representation of action words in the human motor and premotor cortex...' *Neuron* 41:301-307

Hauser, M. and Chomsky, N et al (2002) 'The Faculty of language: What is it, who has it and how did it evolve?' *Science* 298:1569-1579

Heiser, Marc et al (2003) 'The essential role of Broca's area in imitation' *European Journal of Neuroscience* v. 17:5

Hemming, John (2015) *Naturalists in Paradise; Wallace, Bates and Spruce in the Amazon*, (Thames and Hudson)

Higham, Thomas et al (2010) 'Chronology of the Grotte du Renne and implications for the context of ornaments and human remains within the Chatelperronian', *PNAS*: Nov. 107(47)

Higham, Thomas et al (2014) 'The timing and spatiotemporal patterning of Neanderthal disappearance', *Nature:* 512 i. 7514, pp. 306-309

Hikosaka, Okihide et al (2013) 'Why skill matters', *Trends in Cognitive Science* v. 17:9

Hochberg, Julian (1970) *In the Mind's Eye* edited by Mary Petersen et al (Oxford Univ.)

Hoffecker, John F. (2007) 'Representation and Recursion in the Archaeological record', *Journal of Archaeological Method and Theory,* published on line October 17th, 2007

Hölldobler, Bert (2010) 'Multi component signals in ant communication' in *Social Behavior* edited by Tomas Szekely et al, (Cambridge Univ.)

Hsieh, Po-Jang and Tse, Peter U. (2010) 'Brain reading of perceived color reveals a feature mixing mechanism underlying perceptual filling in cortical area VI', *Human Mapping*, (Wiley Liss Inc.)

Hubel, David and Weiss, T. (1986) 'Blobs and Color Vision', Cell Biochemistry and Biophysics', *Proc. Nat'l Acad. Science USA*, 9:1-2:91-102

Hubel, David and Weisel, T. (1965) 'Extent of recovery from the effects of visual deprivation in kittens, '*Journal of Neurophysiology*, 28:1060-72

Hunt, Amelia and Halper, Fred (2008) 'Disorganizing biological motion', *Journal of Vision* v. 12:1-5

Iacobini, Marco and Heiser, Marc et al (2003) 'Short communication: The essential role of Broca's Area in Imitation', *European Journal of Neuroscience,* 17:1123-1128

Ings, Simon, (2007) *A Natural History of Seeing,* (W.W. Norton, New York)

Istomin, Kirill V. and Dwyer, Mark J. (2009) 'Finding the way: A critical discussion of Anthropological theories of human spatial orientation with reference to reindeer herders of Northeastern Europe and Western Siberia', *Current Anthropology,* 50:1:5-28

Istomin, Kiril V. and Dwyer, M.J. (2008) 'Theories of Nomadic Movement: A New Theoretical Approach for Understanding the Movement Decisions of Nenets and Komi Reindeer Herders', *Human Ecology* 36:521

Jakab, Zolton (2003) 'Phenomenal Projection' *Psyche,* 9(04)

Jakab, Zolton (2003B) 'Why not color physicalism without absolutism?' Open peer commentary in *Color realism and Color Science* by Alex Byrne and David Hilbert (Cambridge Univ.)

Jones, Jonathan (2012) *Lost Battles,* (Knopf, New York)

Kandel, Eric (2006) *In Search of Memory*, (W.W. Norton, New York)

Kanwisher, Nancy and Yovel, Galit (2006) 'The fusiform face area: a cortical region specialized for the perception of faces' *Phil. Trans. R. Soc. B.* 361:2109–2128

Kawaura, Satoru, and Tachibanaki, Shuji (2012) 'Explaining the functional differences of rods versus cones', *Focus,* v. 1, Sept/October

Kessler, Klaus and Kiefer, Markus (2005) 'Disturbing visual working memory: Electrophysiological evidence for a role of the prefrontal cortex in recovery from interference,' *Cerebral Cortex,* (Oxford University Press), v. 15, i. 7:1075-1087

Kikyo, H et al (2002) 'Neural correlates for feeling of knowing: an fMRI parametric analysis' *Neuron* 26; 36(1):177-86.

Knoll, Max et al (Jan. 1962) 'Notes on the Spectroscopy of light patterns' *Journal of Analytical Psychology* v. 17 no.1

Koch, Christof and Tsuchiya, N. (2007) 'Attention and consciousness: Two distinct brain processes', *Trends in Cognitive Sciences* v. 11:1, 16-27

Kolb, Helga 'S-Cone pathways' in Webvision, webvision@hsc.utah.edu

Kozhevnikov, Maria et al (2007) 'Spatial visualization in physics problem solving', *Cognitive Sciences*:31, 549-579.

Kozhevnikov, Maria et al (2013) 'Creativity, Visual abilities and visual cognitive styles' *British Journal of Educational Psychology* v. 83, i. 2:196-209

Kuratani, Shigeru (2005) 'Craniofacial development and the development of the vertebrates: The old problems on a new background', *Zoological Science,* 22:1-19

Landman, Rogier and Lamme, Victor (2001) 'Attention sheds no light on the origin of phenomenal experience', *Behavioral and Brain Sciences* 24(5)

Landman, Rogier (2002) 'Large capacity storage of integrated objects before change blindness', *Vision Research* 43 149-164

Lamm, Claus and Singer, Tania (2010) 'The Role of anterior insular cortex in social emotions' in *Brain Structures and Functions* 214:579

Lane, Nick (2000) 'Medical Constraints on the quantum mind', *Journal of the Royal Science of Medicine* v. 93:571-575

Lavin, Claudio et al (2013), 'The anterior cingulate cortex: an integrative hub for human socially-driven interactions', *Frontiers in Neuroscience,* 7:64

Leakey, Richard, (1993) *Origins Reconsidered*, (Random House, New York)

Levy, Daniel (2012) 'Towards an understanding of parietal mnemonic processes: some conceptual guideposts', *Integrative Neuroscience,* v. 6 i. 41

Libet, Benjamin (1985) 'Unconscious cerebral initiative and the role of conscious will in voluntary action', *Behavioral and Brain Sciences 8,* 529-566

Libet, Benjamin, Gleason, C. A., et al (1983). 'Time of conscious intention to act in relation to onset of cerebral activity (readiness- potential). The unconscious initiation of a freely voluntary act.' *Brain*, 106:623-642.

Livingstone, Margaret ((2008) *Vision and Art: The Biology of Seeing,* (Harry Abrams, New York)

Loizos, Caroline (2006 originally published 1967), 'Play Behavior in Higher Primates: A Review', in *Primate Ethology,* ed. by Desmond Morris, 176-218, (New Jersey)

Lynch, Gary and Granger, R. (2008) *Big Brain: The Origins and Future of Human Intelligence*, (Palgrave Macmillan Press, New York)

MacAnany, JJ and Levine, Michael (2004) 'The blanking phenomenon: A novel form of visual disappearance' *Vision Research*

Mamassian, Pasca (2008) 'Ambiguities and conventions in the perception of visual art' *Vision Research* 48:2143-2153

Marcellini, Sara et al (July 2010) 'A modified mark test for our own body recognition in pig tailed macaques', *Animal Cognition,* 13 (4), 631-639

Markovich, Slobodan (?) 'Amodal completion in visual perception' The *Journal* of *General Psychology*, 48, 113-132

Marsh, Lauren et al (2011) 'Disassociation of mirroring and mentalizing systems in autism', *Neuro-image* 30

Mather, George (2005) 'Two-stroke: A new illusion of visual motion based on the time course of neural responses in the human visual system' in *Vision Research,* v. 46 pp. 2015-2018

Matlin, Margaret (2004) *Cognition*, 6th edition, (Wiley)

Macleod, D. and Fine, I. (2001) 'Vision after early blindness', *Journal of Vision,* 1:3
    McDonald, A. J. and Mascagni, F (1997) 'Projections of the lateral entorhinal
    cortex to the amygdala: a Phaseolus vulgaris leucoagglutinin study in the rat'
    in *Neuroscience* v. 77 I2:445-459

Makovsky, Tal and Jiang, Yuhong (2007) 'Distributing versus focusing attention in
    visual short-term memory' *Psychonomic Bulletin and Review* v. 14:6

Melcher, D. & Cavanagh, P. (2011) 'Pictorial cues in art and in visual perception'. Ch.
    19. Francesca Bacci and David Melcher (Eds.), *Art and the senses,* (Oxford, UK:
    Oxford University Press), pp. 359-394

Merzenich, Michael (1983) 'The Reorganization of Somatosensory Cortex following
    peripheral nerve damage in adult and developing mammals' *Annual Review of
    Neuroscience* 6:32S-S6

Miller, J.A. (1987) 'Crazy Quilt Brain', *BioScience* 37:10:701-708

Miyake, Akira, Friedman et al (2002) 'How are visuospatial working memory, executive
    functioning and spatial abilities related? A latent variable analysis' in
    Experimental Psychology: General v. 130 no. 4

Murray, Micah et al, (2004) 'Setting Boundaries: Brain Dynamics of Modal and Amodal
    Illusory Shape Completion in Humans', *The Journal of Neuroscience,* August 4,
    2004 24(31):6898 – 690

Nashner, Lewis (1985) 'Adaptation of human movement to altered environments,' *The
    Motor System in Neurobiology,* edited by Evarts, (Wise and Bousefield, Elsevier
    Bio Medical Press)

Nicholson, Philips T. and Firnhaber, R. Paul (2004) 'Auto hypnotic induction of sleep
    rhythm generates vision of light with form constant patterns' in *Shamansim in
    the Interdisciplinary context,* ed. by Leete and Firnahaber

Novak, Barbara (1980) *Nature and Culture* (Oxford Univ. Press)

Osaka, Naoyuki (2009) 'Walk related mimic words activate the extrastriate visual
    cortex in the human brain: An fMRI Study' *Behavioral Brain Research,* 198:186-
    189

Ostrovsky, Paul et al (2006) 'Vision Following Extended Congenital Blindness'
    Psychological Science, v. 17 no. 121009-1014

Oya, Hiroyuki et al (2002) 'Electrophysiological Responses in the Human
    Amygdala Discriminate Emotion Categories of Complex Visual Stimuli' *The
    Journal of Neuroscience,* 22(21): 9502-9512

Pardo, Jose V. et al (1990) 'The anterior cingulate cortex mediates processing selection
    in the Stroop attentional conflict paradigm', *Proceedings of the National
    Academy of Science,* v. 87:256-259

Passingham, Richard (2009) 'How good is the macaque monkey model of the human brain?', *Current Opinion in Neurobiology,* 19(1):6-11

Pinker, Steven, (2007) ' Toward a consilient study of literature', in *Philosophy and Literature,* v. 31, April:162-178

Pylyshyn, Zenon (2002) 'Mental imagery: In search of a theory' *Behavioral and Brain Sciences,* 25:157-238

Pylyshyn, Zenon (2003) "Return of the mental image: Are there really pictures in the brain?' *Trends in Cognitive Science,* (Rutgers University)

Pryor, Francis, (2008) *Britain: B.C.,* (Harper Perennial)

Purves, Dale et al (2008) *Neuroscience,* (Sinauer Assocs., Sunderland, MA)

Quinn, J.G. (2008) 'Movement and visual coding: The structure of visuo-spatial working memory,' *Cognitive Processing,* v. 9, i. 1:35-43

Rabins, Peter (2013) *Seeking the Why of things* (Columbia Univ. Press)

Renfrew, Colin editor (2009) *Becoming Human, Innovation in Prehistoric Material and Spiritual Culture* (Cambridge University Press)

Rizzolatti, G. (1996) 'Premotor cortex and recognition of motor actions', *Cognitive Brain Research,* 131:41

Roe, Susan (2015) *In Montmartre: Picasso, Matisse and Modernism in Paris 1900-1910,* (Penguin, New York)

Ross, John et al (1997) 'Compression of Visual space before saccades' *Nature* v. 386:597-601

Russell, Richard, Duchaine, Bradley and Nakayama, Ken (2009) 'Super recognizers: People with extraordinary face recognition ability' *Psychonomic Bulletin and Review,* 16:2, pp. 252-257

Sacks, Oliver (1995) *An Anthropologist on Mars,* (Random House, New York)

Saygin, A. P. et al (2004) ' Point-light biological motion perception activates human promotor cortex', *The Journal of Neuroscience,* 24(27):6181-6188

Santos, Michael et al (2011) 'Von Economo neurons in Autism: A stereologic study of the front insular cortex in children', *Brain Research* 1380, 206-217

Schultz, Robert T. (2005) 'Developmental deficits in social perception in autism: the role of the amygdala and fusiform face area' in *International Journal of Developmental Neuroscience* v. 23:2-3:125-141

Seigel, Susannah (2010) *The Contents of visual experience,* (Oxford Univ. Press)

Seitz, Aaron R et al (2005) 'Visual experience can substantially alter critical flicker fusion thresholds' *Human Psychopharmacology Clinical and Experiment Journal* 20:55–60

Shipton, Ceri (2009) 'Imitation and Shared Intentionality in the Acheulean', *Cambridge Archaeological Journal,* 20:2 pp.197-210

Singh, Manish (2004) 'Modal and Amodal Completion Generate Different Shapes' *Psychological Science* v. 15:7

Smith, Denise (2009) 'Style vs Memetics: Exploring some new ideas', *Rock Art Research*, 26:1

Spruston, Nelson (2008) 'Pyramidal Neurons; Dendritic structure and Synaptic integration,' *Neuroscience*, v. 9

Suddendorf, Thomas et al (2009) 'Mental time traveling and the shaping of the human mind' *Philosophical Transactions of the Royal Society* 364:1317–1324

Sutherland, N.S. (1968) 'Outlines of a Theory of Visual Pattern Recognition in Animals and Man', *Proceedings B, The Royal Society*, 171, i. 1024

Studdert-Kennedy, Michael and Goldstein, Louis '*Launching Language: The Gestural Origin of Discrete Infinity*', (Yale University)

Thakkar, Katharine et al (2008) 'Response monitoring, repetitive behavior and anterior cingulate abnormalities in autism spectrum disorders', *Brain,* published by *Oxford Journals,* v. 131 i. 9(a) 2464-2478

Tallon-Baudry, Catherine et al (1999) 'Sustained and transient oscillatory responses in the gamma and beta bands in a visual short-term memory task in humans' *Visual Neuroscience, (*Cambridge University Press) v. 16:449-459

Thomson, Kaivo and Watt, Anthony (2013) 'Investigating cognitive styles differences in the perception of biological motion associated with visuo-spatial processing' *Polish Psychological Bulletin* v. 44(1) 50-55

Todorov, Alexander and Engell, Andrew (2008) 'The role of the amygdala in implicit evaluation of emotionally neutral faces' in *Social Cognitive and Affective Neuroscience* 3:4 303-312

Tomasello, Michael (1999) *The Cultural Origins of Human Cognition* (Harvard University Press, Cambridge)

Tse, Peter Ulrich (1999) 'Volume Completion', *Cognitive Psychology* 39:37-68

Tse, Peter Ulrich (1999) 'Complete mergeability and amodal completion' *Acta Psychologica* 102:165-201

Turner, Jonathan H. and Maryanski, Alexandra (2008) *On the Origin of Societies by Natural Selection,* (Paradigm, London)

Ullsperger, Markus et al (2014) 'Neurophysiology of performance monitoring and adaptive behavior', v. 94 no. 1, 35-79

Ungerleider, Leslie G. et al (1998), 'A neural system for human visual working memory', *Proc. National Acad. of Sciences USA,* 95:3:883-890

Vaina, Lucia and Solomon, J et al (2001) 'Functional Neuroanatomy of Biological Motion Perception in Humans', *PNAS,* (Sept.) 98:20

Valentine, Tim (1991) 'A Unified account of the effects of distinctiveness, inversion and race in face recognition', *Quarterly Journal of Experimental Psychology*, 43A:2:161-204)

Von Humboldt, Wilhelm (1999) *On Language, On the Diversity of Human Language Construction and its Influence on the Mental Development of the Human Species*. Edited by Michael Losonsky, pp. 25-64

Wade, Nicholas and Brozek, J. (2006) *Purkinje's Vision,* Lawrence Erlbaum, London
Wallace, Alfred Russell (1858 - July) 'On the tendencies of varieties to depart indefinitely from the original type' (The Ternate Essay) from the *Linnean Society Proceedings of London*, v. 3

Wallis, T. S. A. and Bex, P.J. (2011) 'Visual crowding is correlated with awareness' *Current Biology,* Feb. 8; 21(3):254–258.

Wallis, T and Arnold, D. (2008) 'Motion-induced blindness is not tuned to retinal speed' *Journal of Vision*, February v. 8 no. 2 article 11

Watson, Karli (2006) '*The Von Economo Neurons: From cells to behavior*' Doctoral Thesis for Cal Tech.

Watson, K.K. et al (2006) 'Dendritic architecture of Von Economo neurons', *Neuroscience,*141:1107-1112

White, Randall (1992) 'Towards an Understanding of Material Representation in Western Europe' *Annual Review of Anthropology*, 21:537-564

White, Randall (2006-2007) *Prehistoric Art,* Lecture Series at New York University

Whiten, A. Goodall, J. et al (2001) 'Charting cultural variation in chimpanzees' in *Behavior*

Williams, Justin (2008) 'Self other relations in social development and autism: multiple roles for mirror neurons and brain bases' in *Autism Research*, v.1 i. 2

Wood, Chip (1997) *Yardsticks*, (Northeast Foundation for Children, Greenfield, MA)

Wolpert, DM and Flannigan, JR (2010)'Motor Learning' *Current Biology* 8;20(11):467-72.

Wyder, Melanie T. (2004), 'Contextual Modulation of Central Thalamic Delay Period Activity: Representation of Visual and Saccadic Goals', *Journal of Neurophysiology*, 91:2628-2648

Xu, Yaoda and Jeong, Su Keun (2015) 'The contribution of human superior intraparietal sulcus to visual short-term memory and perception,' Chapter 4 in *Mechanisms of Sensory Working Memory* edited by Pierre Jolicoeur et al, (Elsevier Press)

Xu, Yaoda (2007) 'The role of the superior intraparietal sulcus in supporting visual short-term memory for multifeatured objects', *Journal of Neuroscience*, v. 27 i. 43

Zimmer, Hubert D. (2008) 'Visual and spatial working memory: From boxes to networks', *Neuroscience and Behavioral Reviews* v. 32:1373-1395

Index

A

Giffords, Gabrielle, 71
Gladstone, William, 126
glasses, 69, 94, 163
Goethe, Johann Wolfgang von, 155
Goldenberg, Georg, 110
Goodall, Jane, 40, 170, 206
graffiti art also. *See under* sigma curves
Grandin, Temple, 13, 39–40, 43, 85, 92, 121–22, 142, 197
graphics, lexical, 56, 101
Graves, Austin, 104

H

habitat, 169, 188
Haidle, Miriam, 115–16, 198
handedness, 155
Hansel and Gretel, 80
haptics, 70, 162, 189
Hauber, Marc, 169
Hauser, Marc D., 113, 198
Helmholtz, Herman von, point light images, 177
hemisphere, right, 44, 180, 187
Henshilwood, Christopher, 35
Henshilwood, Stephen, 77
Heraclitus, 139
Hijabs, 36
hippocampus, 41, 45, 103–6, 160, 173, 180
   Cornu Amonis or CA1, 103-105
historical time, 159
history of art, 92
Hitch, Graham, 108
homeobox gene. *See* symmetry
Homer, 125–27
   Odyssey, 126
   Oínopa, 125–26 also see under 'color'
hominids, 16, 54, 142, 163, 170
   Australopithecus, 142
homologue, human, 110–11
Honey bees, 38, 72
Hubel, David, 17, 61
   neural columns also, 77, 110
   /Weissel, Thorsten, 79
human brains
   extrastriate cortex, 70, 101, 119, 180, 202
human communication, language development, 41–42, 113
   evolution, 115, 170, 196
   eyes, 37, 47, 79, 118, 153
   mother's, 137, 172–73, 190
   language, Wernicke functions, 71

Mesolithic, 156–57
  Gobekli Tepe, 156
  Iconography of, 79, 156
meta-tools, 24, 88, 115
metronomes, 45
Michaelangelo, 87
mimicry, 9, 15, 25, 65, 155, 169, 183, 185
mind's eye, 16, 18, 198
mirroring, 50, 185
  Mirror self-recognition or MSR, 184–85
  reflexes, 112, 170, 181, 184–85, 206
modalities, 59–60
Modernism, 203
Mona Lisa, 32, 141
Mondrian, Piet, 77
monkeys, also see 'Apes' 110–11, 151, 169–71, 185, 201
Montcastle, Vernon, 70
Montmartre, 13, 203
moon, 39, 91
Morris, Desmond, 151, 170, 201
mother's smile also see under 'children', 85, 140
motion
  clips, 50, 137, 139
  intended, 51, 173, 176
  movies, 173
  obvious, 177
  single, 173, 177
motor system, human sensory, 53, 70-72, 103, 138, 142, 161-173, 181-188, 202
muscles, 43, 61, 108, 182
  oscillations, 53, 99, 202 also see Nashner, Lewis

N

Namibia
  Himba of Namibia, 129
navigating, maps, 66, 84, 96, 177
Nefertiti's nose, 141
neocortex, 33, 41, 70, 100, 104, 162
  unstressed actions, 99, 107
Neolithic, 156–57
  circles, megalith, 157
  Gavrinis, France, 156
  Knowth, Ireland, 156
neural
  basis of tool use. *See under* stone tools

Thank You.

www.ingramcontent.com/pod-product-compliance
Lightning Source LLC
Chambersburg PA
CBHW030434290526
45786CB00001B/286